GENOCIDAL WARS, firebombed cities, nuclear explosions, concentration camps, spreading plagues of private blood-letting: this century has seen more than its share of planned and unplanned violence, with prospects of still more to come. Historians of the next century will no doubt record tales of the courageous who struggled to survive its storms of violence: the tunnel builders of the ghettos, determined to outwit those who planned their extermination; the mourning women bearing white scarves stamped with the names of their loved ones, standing in silence in the shadows of a terrorist state; 'ethnically cleansed' men and women, weeping over the destruction of their houses and farms, praying that their conquerors do not raze their crops. These tales will prove remarkable for future generations, but only because of the colossal cruelty the same historians will need to note: the cruelty symbolized by the trenches of the Somme, where soil and flesh were pounded into pink-grey mud; the burning and recycling of corpses into gunpowder to make more skeletons out of future enemies; the dripping flesh and swollen faces inflicted by a bomb whose flash proved brighter than the sun; the torturer armed with prized instruments like electrodes, syringes and the rectoscope, a device used to place gnawing and clawing rats inside the victim; the military officers flinging drugged or murdered bodies of young men and women out of helicopters and planes into the ocean depths below.

Such symbols of this long century of violence are now irrevocably part of our living history. They should not be forgotten and they need therefore to be put in perspective, as some nowadays seek to do by taking refuge in the consoling thesis that after a terrible century of violence the world is now being divided into two parts: a democratic zone of peace, containing the comparatively open and prosperous parliamentary democracies, which form a 'security community' comprising one-seventh of the world's population and most of its power, a community wherein national security calculations, military power and war have ceased to be instruments of politics and civil peace is the norm; and the rest of the world, a zone of violent anarchy, hopelessly entangled in war and warlordism, famine and lawlessness, in which civility and stability are mere words because people's lives are trapped by 'coups and revolutions, civil and international wars, and internal massacres and bloody repression'.[1] For citizens living in the so-called democratic zone of peace, alas, the world is not so neatly subdivided into peaceful and violent zones. Nor can it become so, thanks in part to the links between the two worlds forged by global arms production and the violence-ridden drugs trades. Mass migrations, pauperization and prejudice also ensure that rootlessness, ethnic tensions and violent lawlessness are features of nearly every city of the developed democratic world. It could even be said, paradoxically, that those who live within the so-called democratic zone of peace are as much if

---

[1] Max Singer and Aaron Wildavsky, *The Real World Order: Zones of Peace/Zones of Turmoil*, Chatham, N.J. 1993. The analysis rests heavily upon the proposition that democracies neither go to war with one another nor seriously imagine doing so; evidence for the proposition is adduced in R.J. Rummel's *Understanding Conflict and War*, Beverly Hills, Calif. 1975–81, volumes 1–5.

not *more* troubled by violence than the majority of the world's population. The democratic zone of peace feels more violent because within its boundaries images and stories of violence move ever closer to citizens who otherwise live in peace, due to the risk calculations and safety requirements of insurance companies; the eagerness for publicity of policing authorities; campaigns to publicize violence and to mobilize the criminal process (against rapists and child murderers, for instance); and the development of a global system of communications, parts of which know that violence attracts audiences and which are consequently driven by the editorial maxim, 'If it bleeds, it leads'.

The last factor is particularly important. Thanks in part to high-pressure media coverage, the whole world feels increasingly filled with violence and, according to some, Giuseppe Sacco and Umberto Eco for instance, is forced to recognize that it may now be drifting in the direction of a self-contradictory, multilayered 'new middle ages', marked neither by the spiritual unity of Christendom and papal monarchy nor the secular unity of empire: a world in which the significance of territoriality declines and the range of claimed authorities and conflicting types of legitimation expands dramatically; a world in which there is a marked growth, within the European region, of supranational law which takes precedence over the domestic laws of states without being rooted in popular sovereignty; in which there is a return, in both political and everyday discourse, of the notion of world society and, reminiscent of the *ius gentium intra se* of Spanish theologians and teachers of law, the moral duty to intervene wherever human rights are violated; and a world defined by the spread of plagues of private violence and permanent 'civil war' sanctioned by uncontrolled powers – new warlords, pirates, gunrunners, gangsters, sects – to which the modern state was supposed to put an end.[2]

Democratic theory, attuned as it is to the complex ambiguities of the world, should be suspicious of cosmologies of decline or improvement or regress, and yet, as I argue in this essay, it would be foolish to ignore or marginalize the problem of violence. Among the paradoxes of this long century of violence is the paucity of reflections within contemporary political theory, including democratic theory, on the causes, effects and ethico-political implications of violence, understood (crudely) as any uninvited but intentional or half-intentional act of physically violating the body of a person who previously had lived 'in peace'. There are striking exceptions to this rule, and the interesting fact that, in a heavily male-dominated profession, the topic has been disproportionately treated by women political theorists – Hannah Arendt's reflections on violence are exemplary – confirms it. Informal attempts to discuss the meaning or significance of past theories of violence quickly become bogged in swamps of semantic confusion or political indifference or strong academic preferences for analysing theories of justice, communitarianism or the history of half-dead political languages. While there are certainly plenty of case studies of wars, civil wars and other violent conflicts, political reflection has lagged far behind

---

[2] See Umberto Eco, 'Living in the New Middle Ages', in *Faith in Fakes. Essays*, London 1986, pp. 73–85. The twentieth-century version of the idea that the world is slipping back or sliding forwards into a new and violent medievalism 'without Giotto, Dante, or the inspiration of Christ' is traceable to Guglielmo Ferrero, *Peace and War*, London 1933, p. 96 (translation amended).

empirical events. Of course, the sheer quantity of violence heaped by the twentieth century upon itself is enough to make even the most cheerful philosopher pessimistic, and since 'optimists write badly'(Valéry) and pessimists tend not to write, the silence of those parts of the political theory profession which have been shocked by this century's cruelty is understandable. Elsewhere in the profession, the silence is simply inexcusable, for it is as if professional political theory is incapable of learning to think in pain or even that it has forgotten the experience of pain, that it has succeeded in doing what people normally cannot bring themselves to do: to overcome the animal pity that grips those who witness or hear about the physical suffering of others.

The reasons for this frozen political imagination about violence are manifold and could certainly constitute an essay in itself, if only because the glorification of violence as an end in itself, which was entirely absent from European political thought prior to the bellicose outbursts of the Christian Holy Wars or Crusades, is paradoxically in decline, and because the consequent glum silence about violence rests upon a confused and confusing mélange of unspoken prejudices and significant assumptions. A few still believe that there is no problem of violence exactly because the territorially defined state should, or does in fact, monopolize its means. Sometimes it is said bluntly that the subject of violence properly resides in the specialist provinces of criminology or psychiatry or women's studies or war studies, as if the ongoing concern with violence within the field of political reflection for at least two millennia could somehow be surpassed by modularization. Still other political theorists, especially those living and working in the postimperial democracies, tacitly accept a scandalous rule of democratic politics since Vietnam: the embarrassed reluctance or outright refusal of most politicians, except in rare situations and out of self-interest, to speak publicly of killing zones like Kurdistan, Somalia, Rwanda, or Bosnia-Herzegovina, let alone to drum up public support for military intervention and counterviolence against cruelty in these so-called 'far-off' countries. Then there are those theorists who frankly admit to their unreflected belief in the inevitability of violence as a necessary feature of the human condition. Violence is clothed in an aura of strangeness: its causes and consequences are said either to be understood insufficiently to be amenable to a course of treatment or beyond realistic hope of remedy, especially in extreme circumstances such as coups d'état, revolutions and the jostling and confrontation among armed states. This thoroughly modern belief that violence is inevitable is rarely understood as historically specific, which it most certainly is. Marx's thesis (outlined in *Das Kapital*) that 'in actual history conquest, enslavement, robbery, murder, in brief violence, notoriously play the great part' and his dictum that 'violence is the midwife of every old society pregnant with a new one' are exemplary of a conviction, peculiar to all phases of modernity so far, that violence in some form or another is ineluctably present in human affairs. This modern conviction that 'you can't make an omelette without breaking eggs' (Lenin) or that 'political power grows out of the barrel of a gun' (Mao Tse-tung) may be seen as the secularized offspring of Christian Holy War doctrines, which explains why it was virtually absent from political thought prior to the eleventh century, after which time the old 'just war' insistence that violence must be strictly instrumental, a means that is always in need of an end to justify and place limitations upon it, began to crumble. Finally, there are political theorists who cling to the opposite, equally modern, originally religious presumption that violence is anathema because it violates the principle of the sanctity of human life, a presumption that in practice often dovetails with the belief that as far as possible violence should be hidden away from human eyes, and even sometimes with the conviction (expressed in the theory of democratic zones of peace) that the advanced societies are no longer seriously troubled by violence and that theories of violence are perforce losing their raison d'être. Perhaps this latter attitude helps to explain why memories of certain modern classics on the subject seem to be fading. Who today reads Georges Sorel's syndicalist defence of the workers' movement in *Réflexions sur la violence* (1908); Walter Benjamin's fine essay on law, justice and violence, *Zur Kritik der Gewalt* (1921); or Hannah Arendt's attempt to distinguish violence and power in *On Violence* (1969)? Who reads Frantz Fanon's stirring attack on whitewashing colonialism, *Les Damnés de la terre* (1961), with its insistence that the powerless are entitled to kill their oppressors because to do so is to kill two birds with one stone: the oppressor within and the oppressor without?

The Rediscovery of Civil Society

The same presumption and prejudice against the theorization of violence is curiously evident in the contemporary global renaissance of interest in the theory of civil society. A decade ago, talk of civil society was hardly fashionable, even unwelcome in certain circles. Since then, in the European region and elsewhere, the category has become voguish within the social sciences and public life more generally, helped along by the sense of an end of an era, the unacceptability of tyranny, the disenchantment with *étatisme*, the desirability of certain types of liberty and, it should not be forgotten, the political expedience of talking cynically, for cunning political ends, in this language. The renewal of the language of civil society and the state began in Japan in the 1960s, and it subsequently played a leading role in theoretical and political debates in both halves of Europe, throughout Latin and North America, the Islamic countries and parts of south and east Asia. The concept of civil society is now more widely used than ever before in the history of the modern world, including the century of its birth and maturation (1750–1850), so much so that one would expect a simultaneous renaissance of theorizations of violence, especially considering the old-fashioned, everyday connotations of the word *civil* ('polite, obliging, not rude'; 'not military'), the flourishing of the concept in conditions of libertarian opposition to violence-prone *étatisme* and the little recognized fact that every civil society, past and present, has been plagued by tendencies towards cruelty that openly contradict the *idealtypisch* concept of civil society as a haven of openness, nonviolence, solidarity and justice.

The silence about violence within Ernest Gellner's otherwise excellent *Conditions of Liberty: Civil Society and its Rivals* is symptomatic of the problem. Gellner presents a good summary case for the fundamental contemporary relevance of the state/civil society perspective in the social and political sciences. 'Civil Society' (the phrase is capitalized throughout by Gellner) 'is that set of diverse non-governmental institutions which is strong enough to counterbalance the state and, while not preventing the state from fulfilling its role of keeper of the peace and arbitrator between major interests, can nevertheless prevent it from dominating and atomizing the rest of society.'[3] Gellner has an unfortunate tendency to conflate different forms of civil society and to speak of civil society in economistic and masculinist terms. His thesis that Islam is incapable of achieving civil society sometimes borders on Orientalist prejudice; and his neo-Popperian account of scientific progress misses the elective affinity between postfoundationalist perspectives in philosophy and the social sciences, the attitude of democratic scepticism and the horizontal diversity of forms of life that are characteristic institutional features of any civil society. These weaknesses of Gellner's account are excusable in this context, for they are overshadowed by his clear and powerful point that the contemporary popularity of the term is traceable to the fact that wherever it appears civil society, ideal-typically conceived, is a site of complexity, choice and dynamism, and that it is therefore the enemy of political despotism. Gellner emphasizes that the opposition between civil society and political despotism was especially strong under the crisis-ridden totalitarian regimes of the Soviet type, or what he calls 'Caesaro-Papism-Mammonism', whose main feature was a 'near-total fusion of the political, ideological and economic hierarchies'. Soviet totalitarianism was driven by the avowed aim of creating a new socialist man and woman emancipated from possessive individualism, commodity fetishism and subservience. It manifestly failed to achieve any of these aims. Instead, it cultivated cynical, conformist subjects

[3] Ernest Gellner, *Conditions of Liberty. Civil Society and Its Rivals*, London 1994.

who were skilled at double-talk, 'individualists-without-opportunity' who were rendered incapable of effective enterprise, not least because they were imprisoned in a world 'where it was barely possible – or literally not possible at all – to found a philatelic club without political supervision'.

Then came the *annus mirabilis* 1989. The largely non-violent revolutions that erupted in the central-eastern half of Europe in the autumn of that year put paid to this system. Not only did these 'velvet' revolutions represent a practical victory for the forces of the emerging civil society that confronted the totalitarian regimes of the Brezhnevite or Titoist type; they also vindicated the intellectual shift of emphasis towards the category of civil society. But why did the downtrodden and humiliated – some of them in some countries, at least – find themselves attracted to the utopia of civil society? Why did they come bitterly to resent its absence, to feel its lack as 'an aching void'? Gellner couches his answers primarily in terms of a theory of tradition. We are the fruit of what we desire and endorse. Strivings for civil society have become encoded within our historical traditions. Civil society has become part of our make-up. We actually like it, and therefore have no desire to live under any form of state despotism or tradition-bound communitarianism. 'Civil Society . . . seems linked to our historical destiny', he writes. 'A return to stagnant traditional agrarian society is not possible; so, industrialism being our manifest destiny, we are thereby also committed to its social corollaries.'

It may be objected at this point that Gellner is too strongly tempted to talk in such abstractions as 'we' and that he pays too little attention to the uneven spatial and temporal distribution of the civil society tradition in which he claims we are steeped.[4] I shall skip over these objections, which are potentially weighty, and instead concentrate upon Gellner's closely related, structuralist argument that a civil society is a necessary condition of liberty. Gellner reiterates the familiar point that civil society is not a stifling segmentary community ridden with customs and rituals and other forms of ascribed identity. Civil society 'is based on the separation of the polity from economic and social life' and 'the absence of domination of social life by the power-wielders'. It is exactly this spatial independence of civil society, its ability to act at a distance from political rulers, that enables the subjects of civil society to become confident, self-transforming citizens. Not only does the sheer complexity and diversity of patterns of life within civil society militate against essentialist notions of the human condition ('the inhabitant of Civil Society . . . is radically distinct from members of other kinds of society. He is not *man-as-such* [sic]', writes Gellner). Among the additional charms of civil society is that its multiplicity of activities and standards of excellence fosters the illusion of equality of opportunity and, hence, the struggle for self-improvement. 'Civil Society . . . allows quite a lot of people to believe themselves to be at the top of the ladder, because there are so many independent ladders, and each person can think that the ladder on which he [sic] is well placed is the one that really matters.'

---

[4] See the pathbreaking study of the varying strengths of civil-society traditions in several regions of Europe in Jenö Szücs, *Les Trois Europes*, Paris 1988.

The Problem of Incivility

Gellner's positive characterization of civil society as a realm of freedom correctly highlights its basic value as a condition of democracy: where there is no civil society there cannot be citizens with capacities to choose their identities, entitlements and duties within a political-legal framework. The characterization is nonetheless myopic, indeed symptomatic of a virtually universal habit of the friends of civil society to idealize its untrammelled promotion of citizens' freedom. Various negative tendencies of civil society – ranging from confusions about the limits of party competition and the role of communications media to chronic unemployment and sexual discrimination both inside and outside the home – are not only overlooked. There is also a striking omission from Gellner's account – and every other contemporary account – of what I shall term *the problem of incivility*, the extreme case of which is what I shall call *uncivil society*.

The term 'uncivil society' is strange-sounding, maladroit, at worst a malapropism, at best an anachronism, or so it seems. English-language dictionaries tell us that the word 'uncivility' is now virtually obsolete; that the sixteenth-century adjective 'uncivil' refers to behaviour which is 'contrary to civil well-being' or 'barbarous', 'unrefined', 'indecorous', 'improper', 'unmannerly' and 'impolite'. It was in this sense that country folk spoke of 'bad and uncivill Husbandry' (1632) or Shakespeare instructed one of his characters to command: 'Ruffian: let goe that rude uncivill touch'. This strange-sounding talk of 'uncivility' later became the subject of philosophical and literary analysis, especially during the eighteenth century, during precisely the same period when discourses on 'civil society' (*societas civilis, koinōnia politikḗ, société civile, bürgerliche Gesellschaft, Civill Society, società civile*) were flourishing, and when the traditional meaning of this old concept as a synonym for peaceful, well-ordered political association experienced a lengthy process of disordering and subdivision, such that civil society and the state, traditionally linked by the relational concept of *societas civilis*, came to be seen as different entities. 'Men cannot enjoy the rights of an uncivil and of a civil state together',[5] remarked Edmund Burke, echoing the same philosophic concern with uncivility as his predecessor, the Irish writer Jonathan Swift, himself also a protagonist of the old-fashioned but commonplace eighteenth-century meaning of civil society as a politically well-regulated community devoid of violence.

Swift's preoccupation with the problem of violence contrasts with the odd silence about violence in recent accounts of civil society. His concern is strikingly evident in the records of his frequent journeys through the Irish countryside, during which he often observed that the bulk of its inhabitants was 'uncivil' compared with the refined islands of English-speaking civility of his comprador friends and acquaintances living in town and country mansions. Swift's travel reports conjure up the society of unsafe journeys of the medieval period, when setting out meant making a will (as in the departure of Anne Vercos in Paul Louis Claudel's *L'Annonce faite à Marie*) and travelling itself meant crossing the paths of vagabonds, wild animals and bandits. Swift's

[5] Edmund Burke, *A Letter to John Farr and John Harris, Esqrs., Sheriffs of the City of Bristol, On the Affairs of America* (1777), in *The Works of the Right Honourable Edmund Burke*, London 1899, volume 2, p. 203.

presumption that the English oligarchy was the model of a civil nation is reflected in his descriptions of the summers spent away from his native Dublin, usually in the company of a rural gentry or clergy living in sanctuaries of Anglican refinement and comfort. 'I hate *Dublin*, and love the Retirement here, and the Civility of my Hosts', he wrote to his friend Thomas Sheridan from the estate of Sir Arthur and Lady Acheson, at Markethill, County Armagh in the summer of 1728. Swift liked to think of his times as caught up in a momentous struggle between premodern barbarity and modern civility. The struggle unfolded spatially, resembling a hostile geographic division of territory in which the traveller who moved from the zone of civility into the realm of incivility had the unusual experience of going back in time by rushing forward through space. 'You will find what a quick change I made in seven days from London', he told Alexander Pope after returning to the comfort of his residence in his native Dublin. He described moving 'through many nations and languages unknown to the civilized world. And I have often reflected in how few hours, with a swift horse or a strong gale, a man may come among a people as unknown to him as the Antipodes.' Contact with the unknown uncivilized in an Ireland where 'Politeness is as much a Stranger as Cleanlyness' was both fascinating and repulsive. Swift's description of the village of Kilkenny was typical of his view of Ireland as a land largely filled with bestial, dung-throwing Yahoos: 'a bare face of nature, without houses or plantations; filthy cabins, miserable, tattered, half-starved creatures, scarce in human shape; one insolent ignorant oppressive squire to be found in twenty miles riding; a parish church to be found only in a summer-day's journey, in comparison of which, an English farmer's barn is a cathedral; a bog of fifteen miles round; every meadow a slough, and every hill a mixture of rock, heath, and marsh; and every male and female, from the farmer, inclusive to the day-labourer, infallibly a thief, and consequently a beggar, which in this island are terms convertible.'[6]

These observations about uncivility echoed the much older principle of civility elaborated in sixteenth-century Italian courts and seventeenth-century Parisian salons. According to this positive principle, the everyday interactions of men may, in such matters as commerce and love, not only be freed from the threat of violence – from incivility – but also become a source of pleasure. The *natural* potential for aggression among individuals and groups may be overcome by *artificial* conventions, such as refined speech, polite manners, effeminate styles of dress (wigs with long curls, jewels, ribbons, sinuously high-heeled pumps), all of which serve to distance individuals from uncivil habits variously dubbed rustic, crude, rude or unpolished. During this period, the French verb *civiliser* was used to name this process. *Civiliser* is 'to bring to civility, to make manners mild and civil' under 'good government' and 'good laws'.[7] Mirabeau's *L'Ami des hommes ou Traité de la population* (1756), the first French text to use the new-fangled

---

[6] The quotations are respectively from letters written by Jonathan Swift to the Reverend Thomas Sheridan (Market-hill, 2 August 1728); to Alexander Pope (Dublin, August 1726); to Miss Esther Vanhomrigh (7 August 1722); and to Dean John Brandreth (30 June 1732), in *The Correspondence of Jonathan Swift*, Harold Williams, ed., Oxford 1962–72, volume 3, p. 296; volume 3, p. 158; volume 2, p. 433; and volume 4, p. 34.

[7] See Edmond Huguet, *Dictionnaire de la langue française du seizième siècle*, Paris 1925, volume 2, p. 302.

word *civilisation*, added that those who enjoyed a reputation for civility were considered exemplars of 'confraternity' or *sociabilité*; they were 'polished' men whose hearts had been softened, deflected from the temptations of taking violent revenge against others.

There was by no means general agreement in this period that the contemporary struggle against uncivility was a good thing. The invention of civility as an antidote to uncivility was synonymous with controversy. There were, for example, abundant complaints about the hypocrisy of civility, in particular because of the ways in which it served as a mask for the conniving egoism and violence of men with a reputation for refined manners. Mahatma Gandhi's famous remark that the idea of British civilization would be a good one stands towards the end of a long line of complaints of this sort, of which Jean-Jacques Rousseau's sarcastic, savage attack on Hobbes and modern civil society is among the most famous:

> I open the books on Right and on ethics; I listen to the professors and jurists; and, my mind full of their seductive doctrines, I admire the peace and justice established by the civil order; I bless the wisdom of our political institutions and, knowing myself a citizen, cease to lament I am a man. Thoroughly instructed as to my duties and my happiness, I close the book, step out of the lecture room, and look around me. I see wretched nations groaning beneath a yoke of iron. I see mankind ground down by a handful of oppressors. I see a famished mob, worn down by sufferings and famine, while the rich drink the blood and tears of their victims at their ease. I see on every side the strong armed with the terrible powers of the Law against the weak.[8]

---

[8] Jean-Jacques Rousseau, 'Fragments of an Essay on the State of

There were also attempts – well-illustrated by Jonathan Swift's later questioning of English civility in defence of Irish independence – to turn the tables on the powerful by emphasizing that their civility was the ally of arrogance, that it had the unintended effect of producing and reproducing incivility among the powerless, the key implication being that the powerful must somehow change their ways and let the 'uncivilized' find their own path to civility.

Despite such reservations and qualifications, the threat (and fear) of violence always seems to have been lurking behind the concern with civility. Uncivility was the ghost that permanently haunted civil society. In this respect, civilization was normally understood as a project charged with resolving the permanent problem of discharging, defusing and sublimating violence; uncivility was the permanent enemy of civil society. Civilization therefore denoted an ongoing historical process, in which civility, a static term, was both the aim and the outcome of the transformation of uncivil into civil behaviour. From this thesis it was merely a short step from the thought that the civilizing process was a march through stages of gradually increasing perfection. During the eighteenth century, the word 'civilization' connotes both a fundamental process of history and the end result of that process, in which the distinction between the advances of present-day civilization and the actual or hypothetical primitive primordial state (called variously nature, barbarism, rudeness or savagery) becomes ever clearer. The privileged classes of Europe represent themselves as treading a path stretching from primitive

War' (written circa 1752), in *A Lasting Peace through the Federation of Europe and the State of War*, London 1917, pp. 124–5.

barbarism through the present condition of humanity to perfection through education and refinement.

The journey towards civilization is seen to be a slow but steady elimination of violence from human affairs, as Adam Ferguson, influenced by lectures delivered by Adam Smith in 1752, emphasized when first using the word 'civilization' in English. The process of civilization is described as progress from rudeness to refinement, in which the contemporary 'civil society' is understood as a 'polished' and 'refined' form of society with 'regular government and political subordination'. Ferguson emphasized that 'the epithets of *civilized* or of *polished*' properly refer to 'modern nations', which differ from '*barbarous* or *rude*' nations principally because of their discretionary use of violence. In barbarous nations, Ferguson insisted, 'quarrelling had no rules but the immediate dictates of passion, which ended in words of reproach, in violence, and blows'. Tides of violence flooded the field of government as well. 'When they took arms in the divisions of faction, the prevailing party supported itself by expelling their opponents, by proscriptions, and bloodshed. The usurper endeavoured to maintain his station by the most violent and prompt executions. He was opposed, in his turn, by conspiracies and assassinations, in which the most respectable citizens were ready to use the dagger.' Barbarous nations were equally rude in the conduct of war. 'Cities were razed, or inslaved; the captive sold, mutilated, or condemned to die.' By contrast, Ferguson observed, civilized or polished nations had gone some way in extruding crudely violent scenes from the stage of contemporary life. 'We have improved on the laws of war, and on the lenitives which have been devised to soften its rigours,' wrote Ferguson. 'We have mingled politeness with the use of the sword; we have learned to make war under the stipulations of treaties and cartels, and trust to the faith of an enemy whose ruin we meditate.' Civilized societies are guided by the principle of 'employing of force, only for the obtaining of justice, and for the preservation of national rights.'[9]

The Civilizing Process

Among the weaknesses of this type of eighteenth-century interpretation of the problem of violence and civil society is its secret commitment to an evolutionary or teleological understanding of history as a process of transformation from 'rude' societies to 'civilized' societies. Ferguson himself worried about the possible relapse into barbarism, but the general framework of his study stands firmly on the assumption that modern times differ from and are superior to previous eras of rudeness because violence is potentially removable from significant areas of life. The evolutionary assumption is explicit in the works of other Scottish colleagues of Ferguson – such as James Dunbar's *Essays on the History of Mankind in Rude and Cultivated Ages* (1780) and John Logan's *Elements of the Philosophy of History* (1781) – who treat of violence as the antithesis of civil society and assume, optimistically, that it is on the wane in modern civil societies. This unexplained optimism is of

[9] Adam Ferguson, *An Essay on the History of Civil Society*, Edinburgh 1767; especially part 1, section 4 ('Of the Principles of War and Dissension'), pp. 29–37; part 2 ('Of the History of Rude Nations'), pp. 112–64; and part 3, section 6 ('Of Civil Liberty'), pp. 236–56.

interest and consequence, since precisely the same premise is invisibly at work in latter-day theorizations of civil society. I am convinced that this premise is rendered both questionable and undesirable not only by the patterns of terrible crimes of state violence committed throughout the twentieth century, but also by the fact that it serves to distract our attention from three other basic facts of the long century of violence now drawing to a close: the chronic persistence of violence *within* all extant civil societies; the (not unrelated) permanent possibility that civil societies can and do regress into *uncivil* societies; and the (again related) long-term growth, for the first time on any scale, of a new *politics of civility* aimed at publicizing and reducing the incidence of such disparate phenomena as murder and rape, genocide and nuclear war, the violence of disciplinary institutions, cruelty to animals, child abuse and capital punishment.

Within the twentieth-century social sciences, Norbert Elias did more than anybody to stimulate awareness of some of these points. His discussion of the strengths – and weaknesses – of the so-called civilizing process represents a pathbreaking attempt to counter the post-nineteenth century's loss of interest in and neglect of the topic of civility, and his effort, which is comparable in scope and intention with the older work of Rondelet, Tocqueville and others,[10] is of vital importance to a theorization of violence and civil societies. His *Über den*

[10] See C. Haroche, 'La Civilité et la politesse – des objets négligés de la sociologie politique', *Cahiers internationaux de sociologie*, volume 94, 1993, pp. 97–120. The key work of Norbert Elias referred to here is *Über den Prozess der Zivilisation. Soziogenetische und psychogenetische Untersuchungen*, 2 volumes, Basel, 1939.

Prozess der Zivilisation (1939) proposed that from the sixteenth century onwards, particularly in the upper-class circles of the courteoisie, social standards of conduct and sentiment began to change drastically. Codes of conduct became stricter, more differentiated and all-embracing, but also more even, more temperate, banishing excesses of self-castigation as well as of self-indulgence. Spontaneous behaviour was repressed; men who once ate from the same dish or drank from the same cup or spat in each other's presence were separated by a new wall of restraint and embarrassment at the bodily functions of others; physical impulses (such as farting, defecating and urinating) were checked by self-imposed prohibitions and subjected to new rules of 'privacy'; prudery came to surround wedding ceremonies, prostitution and discussions of sexual matters; language became more delicate. Even death itself became an embarrassment to the living. To express pleasure in violence, whether in mutilating one's opponents in battle or in burning cats alive (an annual ceremony in Paris), came to be regarded as rude and repulsive. Elias shows that this transformation was closely related to the process of state formation, particularly the subjection of the warrior classes to stricter control and the 'courtization' of the nobles. The whole process found its expression in a new term launched by Erasmus of Rotterdam, the term 'civility', which later gave rise to the verb 'to civilize', both of which were soon used in many other countries as a symbol of the new struggle to refine and polish manners.

Elias argues that the civilizing process, which he does *not* understand as synonymous with Europe or the West, is best understood as a fragile historical episode linking the medieval and contemporary modern worlds. Elias criticizes the tendency to use the term normatively, as if it were synonymous with the triumphs and achievements of modern Europe in the wider world. He comments:

> In 1798, as Napoleon sets off for Egypt, he shouts to his troops: 'Soldiers, you are undertaking a conquest with incalculable consequences for civilization.' Unlike the situation when the concept was formed, nations from hereon consider the process of civilization as completed within their own societies; they see themselves as bearers of an existing or finished civilization to others, as standard-bearers of civilization in foreign lands. Of the whole preceding process of civilization nothing remains in their consciousness except a vague residue. Its impact is understood simply as an expression of their own higher gifts; the fact that, and the question of how, during the course of many centuries, their own civilized behaviour has been formed is of no interest.[11]

Elias correctly warns against this amnesia and its pompous political consequences. His warning could have more sting if it were tougher on the superiority complex of the European mode of civilization, for instance, or if it adopted a more rigorously sceptical attitude towards certain *apparent* civilizing trends. Elias's work contains something of an implicitly progressive view of the growth of modern patterns of civility, symptomatic of which is his general neglect of the ways (outlined by Foucault and others) in which a civilizing process may redeploy, sanitize and camouflage disciplinary and other violence without necessarily diminishing it. The nineteenth-century reduction of capital offences and the abolition of public hangings in 1868 in England,

---

[11] Elias, *Über den Prozess der Zivilisation*, volume 1, p. 63.

for example, can hardly be attributed to the growing practical triumph of liberal civility.[12] Prosecutions and capital convictions had risen so dramatically by the early nineteenth century that by the 1830s more than 90 per cent of death sentences were not carried out lest the English landscape be clogged with gibbets, and not because of mounting humanitarian sympathy for the condemned. Similarly, the privatization of hangings, from the abolition of the Tyburn procession in 1783 to the dismantling of scaffolds inside prison walls in 1868, had little to do with a principled commitment to civility. The transfer of executions indoors, the hiding away of violence from the public eye, was sometimes seen by its advocates as a means of dampening public attacks on the whole dirty business of capital punishment. Hanging arguably also became more cruel since felons were denied the active sympathy formerly extended to them by onlookers. Those whose hourglasses had been turned for the last time were now left to face death alone, in the hope – pious Anglicans calculated – that their sinful souls would repent.

Elias nevertheless remains adamant: those Europeans who consider themselves the bearers of civilization resemble a tiny, courtly, aristocratic upper class lording over the rest of the world, an enclave falsely proud of their achievements, despite clear evidence that *other* civilizations – I shall not elaborate this point – have long enjoyed sophisticated methods of pacification and despite the fact, Elias adds, that the originally European mode of civilization is potentially self-paralysing. This emphasis upon the *self-destructive limits* of the civilizing process is

[12] V.A.C. Gatrell, *The Hanging Tree. Execution and the English People, 1770–1868*, Oxford 1994.

particularly important because it highlights an exogenous source of incivility in civil societies. Elias's thesis can be put briefly: the modern civilizing process is directly related to the formation and growth of states seeking to disarm competitor power groups and thereby monopolize the means of violence over a given territory and its inhabitants. The creation of the modern state – an impersonal, abstract entity that stands above and is distinct from both the government of the day and the governed – is synonymous with the erection of a sovereign and therefore indivisible power apparatus, the *defensor pacis* as Marsilius of Padova called it, that puts an end to social violence by wielding a monopoly of armed force over a population that enjoys freedom from everyday violence precisely because it agrees, more or less, to regard the state's monopoly of violence as legalized violence.

Such concentrations of the physical means of violence, which are normally controlled and managed by governments, backed up by the military and police as their executive organs, are, like so many other human inventions, highly equivocal. According to Elias, just as the taming of fire favoured progress in the cooking of food as well as the barbarian burning down of huts and houses, so the invention of states that exercise a monopoly of physical violence is an equally ambiguous innovation. States are positively dangerous instruments of pacification. On the one hand, within their given territories, they are peace-enforcing and peace-keeping agencies. The peace enjoyed by political subjects assumes the form of state-controlled and legalized violence, which releases individuals and groups from the hellish reality (in Hobbes's famous words) of 'continuall feare, and danger of violent death; And the life of man, solitary, poore, nasty, brutish, and short'. The exercise of violence consequently becomes, at least in principle, predictable and controllable. And yet, on the other hand, the modern process of state-secured pacification is not extended to the relationships *among* states, which, despite interstate negotiations, diplomacy and peace agreements, continue to be caught up in a *bellum omnium contra omnes*. The modern state is too civil by half. 'As in every system of balances with mounting competition and without a central monopoly, the powerful states forming the primary axes of tensions within the system force each other in an incessant spiral to extend and strengthen their power position.'[13] That means that war, whose essence is violence, the sparing use of which under battle conditions is imbecility, constantly threatens both particular states' monopoly of the means of violence (in that they can be defeated militarily by their enemies abroad or by civilian unrest at home) and the nonviolent civil conditions enjoyed by their subjects. Elias's point is that the power of deploying the means of violence in the hands of a few and for the benefit of certain small groups can be used to make war on other states and their populations. War and rumours of war are omnipresent conditions of the civilizing process.

Those who enjoy the monopoly of the means of violence can also turn their life-threatening power against their own subject populations. Rousseau's remark that 'the whole life of kings, or of those on whom they shuffle off their duties, is devoted solely to two objects: to extend their rule beyond their frontiers and to make it more absolute within them'[14] applies to the whole of

---

[13] Elias, *Über den Prozess der Zivilisation*, volume 2, p. 435.

[14] Jean-Jacques Rousseau, 'A Lasting Peace through the Federation of Europe' (1756), in *A Lasting Peace through the Federation of Europe and the State of War*, p. 95.

the modern period of states and state-building. While premodern political systems normally attempted to ensure the obedience of their subjects and extract from them as much wealth as possible, they frequently lacked the resources for pulverizing and dominating the societies they attempted to control. They consequently resorted to the paradoxical strategy of allowing local communities and whole regions both to administer themselves and supply money, produce or corvée labour, on pain of punishment. The modern state, by contrast, functions as an instrument of domination with concentrated armed force at its centre. It does so because at an earlier point in its history it disarmed autonomous feudal lords, communal militias, mercenaries, pirates and duelling aristocrats. The modern state is therefore potentially more terrible in its effects than premodern political systems. Its monopoly of the means of violence, as Hobbes remarked, places its subjects permanently under a cloud of threatened violence.

Elias is right to observe that state violence can and has often destroyed civility, leaving in its wake social relations riddled with incivility: violence, insecurity, aggravated conflict, old scores to be settled tomorrow or the day after. Dozens of contemporary societies around the world are currently suffering such symptoms, but there are scores of earlier recorded cases of overly strong and expansionist centralized states undercutting the ability of subjects to organize themselves into nonviolent, intermediary associations. From the time of the first wars linked to the state-building process in the Italian Renaissance and the violent destruction of religious groupings like the Huguenots by the French monarchy in the sixteenth and seventeenth centuries, violent rulers have gutted their respective societies and robbed populations of their capacity for peaceful self-organization except for kinship groups or state-sponsored organizations. Elias himself highlights this state production of barbarism in a chilling account of the Freikorps revenges in the Baltic area after Versailles. Pressured by entente and the peace treaty, the Berlin government ordered the withdrawal of German troops from the Baltic region. Many resentful Freikorps refused. They stayed and fought on, not against the Red Army, which had already retreated, but against reorganized Estonian and Latvian troops backed by British warships. The barbarism that ensued is illustrated by Elias with a citation from the diary of a Freikorps officer:

> We fired into surprised crowds, and raged and shot and struck and hunted. We drove the Latvians across the fields like rabbits and set fire to every house and blasted every bridge to dust and cut every telegraph pole. We threw the corpses into the wells and threw in hand grenades. We killed whoever we captured, we burned whatever would burn. We saw red, we no longer had any human feelings in our hearts. Wherever we had camped, the ground groaned under our destruction. Where we had stormed, where formerly houses had stood, there now lay rubble, ashes, and glimmering beams, like abscesses in the bare fields. A huge trail of smoke marked our paths. We had ignited a huge pile of wood, which burned more than dead matter. On it burned our hopes, our desires: the bourgeois tablets, the laws and values of the civilised world, everything that we had dragged along with us as moth-eaten rubbish, the values and faith in the things and ideas of the time that had abandoned us. We pulled back, boasting, exhilarated, loaded with booty.[15]

[15] Norbert Elias, 'Violence and Civilization: the State Monopoly

Such details of the slide into barbarism are frightening. They proved to be not only the prelude to something that had never happened before – the chillingly efficient, well-organized extermination of millions in gas chambers and ovens – but also an anticipation of thousands of recorded twentieth-century instances in which the wielders of state violence devoured all remnants of civility, along with their subjects. Future political historians of the twentieth century will hopefully recall what are surely among the most bizarre cases of this potential for extreme violence by (would-be) officials of the modern state: the systematic rape of women by soldiers, often with terrified local men forced at gunpoint to look on; the ritual mutilation of victims, such as cutting off their noses, breasts, ears or penises; and the practice of forcing members of a family group at knife- or gunpoint to kill each other (slowly) in turn, or even to force parents to maim or kill or hack their children to pieces, and to cook and eat the prepared dish prior to their own execution.[16] These cases of violence are grotesque reversals of Claude Lévi-Strauss's dictum that primitive cultures are *anthropophagic* (they 'devour' their adversaries) while modern civilizations are *anthropoemic* (they segregate, evict, marginalize or 'vomit' their adversaries), but it would be mistaken to conclude that they somehow represent a lapse into 'traditionalism' or 'tribalism'. They are in fact quintessentially modern, not

---

of Physical Violence and Its Infringement', in John Keane, ed., *Civil Society and the State. New European Perspectives*, London and New York 1988, pp. 196–7 (my translation).

[16] All of these practices are documented in K.B. Wilson, 'Cults of Violence and Counter-Violence in Mozambique', *Journal of Southern African Studies*, volume 18, number 3, September 1992, pp. 527–82.

only because of their implication in the struggle for territorially bound state power, but also because they are illustrations of the rational-calculating use of violence as a technique of terrorizing and demoralizing whole populations and preventing them from engaging in organized or premeditated resistance. An extreme version of this modernist use of exemplary violence to cow and control the state's subjects was evident in the Central African Republic regime operated by Jean-Bedel Bokassa, who himself was renowned for ordering on one occasion the murder of fellow ministers, politicians, officials and army officers; personally murdering several dozen children who were disappeared after protesting against school uniforms; and practising cannibalistic rites, in the process filling his Kologa Palace fridges with human corpses stuffed with rice in preparation for eating.

The Limits of Barbarism

IT WOULD BE possible at this stage of reflection on violence to draw the pessimistic conclusion that civil societies cannot escape the monopolistic powers of the sovereign state, within whose shadow, as Elias's humbling account implies, each newborn child is today expected within a few years to do what is virtually impossible: to acquire a sense of non-violent self-control, shame and delicacy which it has taken European populations many centuries to develop. Zygmunt Bauman's *Modernity and the Holocaust* presents the most sophisticated version of this line of argument. Previous theorists of the modern European civilizing process, Elias included, are charged with ignoring the perversely self-destructive dynamic of violence. The modern civilizing process, typically understood as the slow but steady inculcation of shared norms such as the abhorrence of murder, the disinclination to violent assault, moral responsibility for one's actions in the world and the fear of a guilty conscience, not only results (as Elias concedes) in dangerous concentrations of the means of violence in state hands; it is *also* a process of insulating the ownership and deployment of violence against moral calculations and, hence, carries within it the seeds of planned cruelty on a mass scale. The civilizing process logically leads to the kind of amoral attitude displayed by Dr Servatius in his summary defence of Adolf Eichmann in Jerusalem: figures like Eichmann are decorated for acts if they triumph over their enemies, whereas they go to the gallows in disgrace if they are defeated. It follows from this phenomenon of amoral violence, Bauman argues, that zones of civility in everyday life are possible only because somewhere in the wings physical violence is stored up in institutional places and quantities that effectively place it beyond the control of ordinary citizens. Everyday codes of conduct thus mellow mainly because the subjects of state power are constantly threatened with violence in case they are violent – with violence they themselves cannot match or reasonably expect to repulse. The pacification of everyday life renders most people defenceless; they become the playthings of the potentially sinister managers of coercion. In effect, Bauman's thesis is the mirror image of the late-eighteenth-century view of the civilizing process as an upward spiral into civility. Civility and barbarity lie side by side on a down-spiralling continuum of violence. There is, he claims, no dividing line between civilized norms and uncivil abnormality. Civilization should be a synonym for the constant potential, under modern conditions, of political power perfecting itself into the bureaucratic planning and execution of genocide. 'Holocaust-style phenomena must be recognized as legitimate outcomes of [the] civilizing tendency, and its constant potential.'[17]

Bauman is surely right to insist – here he rewords a key thesis in post-Weberian sociological theory in Germany – that totalitarianism is no mere accident on the super-highway of modern progress. His thesis also helpfully points to one of the most disturbing enigmas that any political theory of violence must face: that there are times and places when civilized manners can and do peacefully cohabit with mass murder. Among the bizarre twentieth-century examples of this enigma (unmentioned by

---

[17] Zygmunt Bauman, *Modernity and the Holocaust*, Oxford 1993, especially pp. 12–18, 27–30, 107–11.

Bauman) is the *Great Gatsby*-style party, held in late April 1935 in Moscow, hosted by the first American Ambassador to the Soviet Union, William C. Bullitt, when, at precisely the time that the purges were reaching frenzied proportions, the entire Soviet elite, bar Stalin himself, reportedly socialized with smiling faces, cigarettes and drinks in hand, knowing that the guests included henchmen and victims, many of whom were both. The same bizarre type of occasion, in which civility greets barbarity, is symbolized by the friendly, relaxed atmosphere at Wannsee in January 1942, where Müller, Heydrich, Eichmann and his Nazi colleagues sipped champagne and smoked cigars after a hard day's work deciding the details of how to proceed with the *Endlösung*; and it is typified by the civilized trials of war criminals at Nuremberg, a city that lay in ruins carpeted by tens of thousands of corpses, whose rotting flesh made local water dangerously undrinkable, as if it were water trickling from a morgue.

These points made by Bauman are salutary, and yet his conclusion that modern civility is the ally of barbarity has its costs, one of which is his dogmatic pessimism. The postulates of 'mutual assistance, solidarity, reciprocal respect etc.', qualities to which Bauman pays lip service (since they are antithetical to totalitarianism) and which are normally considered among the organizing principles of any functioning civil society, are brushed aside conceptually as mere phantoms; in other words, civil society, a category that Bauman needs to rescue modernity from itself, is subjected to a reductionist interpretation that, formally speaking, resembles the Marxian reduction of civil society to bourgeois domination and violence. Not surprisingly, Bauman's conclusions slip into moroseness.

The type of analysis of 'modern civility as barbarity' proffered by Bauman also misses the point that the modern civilizing process contains several potentially productive – if dangerous – contradictions. One of them is the frightening development of techniques of total war and universally devastating means of violence that threaten the very capacity of states and their subjects to secure themselves against the ravages of war. Mechanized total war is an invention of the late eighteenth century that only reached perfection – and the height of self-contradiction – during our long century of violence. Born of all-devouring confrontations at sea, in which the aim is skilfully to destroy one's opponents and their equipment completely, total war, according to Admiral Friedrich Ruge, aimed 'at destroying the honour, the identity, the very soul of the enemy'. During the 1930s, Lieutenant-General von Metsch agreed: 'In total war, everything is a front! But along with the new total front, we would be wise to include *the nation's spiritual front*. . . . In both the practical matter of preparation for rearmament and theoretical military discussions, the moral question is of primary importance.'[18] It evidently never occurred to von Metsch that 'the moral question' would produce surprising answers, centring especially on the topic of whether war, or at least certain types of war, is still possible in a world flooded with weaponry, some of which, if used by their respective combatants, would necessarily catapult us from, say, the early-nineteenth-century world of Colonel Shrapnel testing his deadly new fragmenting shell on the wildlife of Foulness Island, into a world in which the use of the

[18] Cited in Paul Virilio, *Speed and Politics. An Essay on Dromology*, New York 1986, p. 75.

latest weapons of war would render (certain forms of) war obsolete, simply because human beings, let alone armies and weapons systems, could no longer continue to exist anywhere on the face of the earth, or at least in certain of its formerly populous regions.

The history of the development of modern weapons systems was from the outset pregnant with this possibility that violence begets violence and so threatens the utility of violence. Michael Howard's fine study of the growth of weapons of violence in Europe pinpoints a number of episodes in which the invention of a new weapon paralyses the ability of the combatants to fight a war effectively.[19] In 1346, in the battle at Crécy, Edward III introduced longbow archers against enemy cavalry. These longbows which shot five or six arrows in the same period of time that an old-fashioned crossbow took to shoot just one of its darts, devastated their opponents; according to reliable estimates, more than fifteen thousand of them were killed for about a hundred English casualties. Thereupon, cavalry commanders everywhere became convinced that their men-at-arms must don heavier plate armour, the net effect of which (as the French discovered to their cost at Poitiers in 1356 and Agincourt in 1415) was to render cavalrymen *on both sides* useless when dismounted and incapable of speedy or clear-sighted manoeuvres when mounted. This same self-contradictory logic of obsolescence within the modernization of weapons, whose propensity to devastate and kill grows exponentially, precisely because that is their purpose, became evident again during the twentieth century. Long before Hitler's rise to

[19] Michael Howard, *War in European History*, London, Oxford and New York 1976, pp. 11–12.

power, for instance, the *Reichswehr* command had formulated a strategy for taking advantage of the latest weapons of war by drawing up detailed plans for the defence of Germany against a possible French invasion.[20] It recommended that in such circumstances Germany and the Germans would have to be treated like a subject African colony. Every bridge, road and telephone line would have to be destroyed; mustard gas bombs would need to be dropped on German citizens to hinder the French advance; and it would be necessary to wage semi-permanent guerrilla operations without regard for the distinction between civilians and armies.

The bizarre logic of total war evident in the German generals' insistence that Germany might have to be destroyed in order to save it may be said to have reached its apogee with the invention and deployment of nuclear weaponry, the destructive potential of which is symbolized by the dripping flesh, swollen faces and molten and con-fused bodies left behind on the scorched earth of Hiroshima by the swooping Enola Gay one summer's day early in August 1945. Since that day, the principle of annihilation, which recognizes no 'class principle' (Khrushchev), has bedevilled the whole world; the human species has had to contend not only with its own individual mortality but the possibility of the collective death of humanity. The number of nuclear-tipped states has continued to grow, and there is no end to talk of the benefits and necessary evil of nuclear weaponry, despite a growing body of sober warnings about their dangerously self-contradictory potential.

Nervous arguments for and against nuclear weapons

[20] See W. Deist, ed., *The German Military in the Age of Total War*, Leamington Spa 1985, p. 123.

are sometimes combined in assessments of the post-Cold War world, in the scholarly but self-contradictory proposals for 'minimal nuclear pluralism' developed by Singer and Wildavsky, for instance.[21] They yearn for a tripolar world in which, ideally, the United States, China and a combined European nuclear force (comprising the weaponry of Britain, France and the former Soviet Republics) together exercise strict oligopolistic control over the development and deployment of nuclear arsenals for the ultimate purposes of expanding the democratic zone of peace and creating a safer 'non-nuclear world'. Nuclear weapons are not especially dangerous, and they are for the time being a necessity, they say. The 'natural' condition of nuclear weapons is to be unused, and, besides, there are clearly definable defensive benefits accruing to states tipped with nuclear weapons, since their potential nonnuclear enemies are forced to think twice about the probable consequences of military engagement. The cost to the big powers of developing effective shields against would-be nuclear competitors is not especially prohibitive, and in any case, they add, the negative consequences of using nuclear weapons in battle have been exaggerated by their critics. 'While fallout would cause many deaths outside the zone of combat if large numbers of weapons were exploded near the ground', they claim, 'the numbers would not be large compared to the number of people otherwise dying of diseases and accidents and would not substantially change people's life expectancy in any country not in the war itself.'

Given these strongly worded considerations, it is perhaps surprising that Singer and Wildavsky ultimately

[21] Singer and Wildavsky, *The Real World Order,* pp. 60–76.

remain unconvinced of their own confident claims, but the confusion of their case is in fact expressive of the very nuclear contradiction they want to wish away. They admit that even though the maintenance of nuclear forces is expensive, cost considerations and arms-control agreements are proving incapable of preventing states of every description from acquiring the technical capability of building nuclear weapons. Besides, the two basic forms of missile defence systems, the space-based 'brilliant pebbles' method of filling the heavens with orbiting satellites trained to collide with airborne ballistic missiles, or the 'brilliant eyes' method of using ground-based interceptors, have their technical limitations; they also remain vulnerable to the clandestine delivery of weapons of mass destruction (suitcase bombs) by means of ships or as airfreight. Moreover – the honest reasoning of Singer and Wildavsky becomes powerful here – the more countries that have nuclear weapons, the more probable it is that some nuclear weapons will be used by 'desperate, irresponsible, or crazy' governments, or escape from governmental control and fall into the hands of groups that might either have an accident with them or actually use them. Then there is the ultimate risky fact about the bomb:

> Nuclear weapons have the possibility of getting out of control. Countries can produce thousands of them. They can be made very large. Through unimaginable circumstances, there can be wars in which many thousands of them are used and hundreds of millions of people are killed. Even though this is extremely unlikely, the possibility is inherent in the nature of nuclear weapons.

This self-contradiction within the 'realist' logic

governing the interaction of heavily armed nation-states hellbent on permanent rearmament – that it strikes down von Clausewitz's dictum that victory in modern warfare goes to the side that can will itself to survive and persuade its adversary to surrender – might be described as an instance of what I shall call the paradox of Damocles. It is well known that in the court of Dionysius, the terrible tyrant ruler of Syracuse during the fourth century BC, there was a courtier named Damocles. Even though Dionysius heaped cruelty onto all his subjects, who hated him in return, Damocles praised the ruler's greatness, agreed with all his opinions and laughed at everything the despot found funny. Damocles's only regret was a wish: to become a ruler just like the violent Dionysius. The tyrant was no fool, and easily spotting the crude flattery of his simpleton subject, he decided to teach Damocles a lesson by commanding him to dress in royal garments and a gold crown, and to preside as ruler at a magnificent banquet held in his honour. Damocles was overjoyed, but his mood changed suddenly when he discovered, hanging by a single hair immediately above his throne, a huge sharpened sword aimed directly at the centre of his head. Damocles cried out in horror, begging to be seated with the rest of the guests, but Dionysius at first refused. Before hurrying off the throne, greatly relieved, his foolish courtier had to be taught a fundamental (if paradoxical) lesson about state violence: since those who rule by the sword potentially die by the sword, those who govern, or have designs on government, are best advised to seek means other than violence through which to command the allegiance of their subjects.

The flight of Damocles serves as a reminder that the history of modern state building is more complicated than scholars such as Elias and Bauman have supposed, and that the development of an international system of states struggling to monopolize the means of violence within a clearly delimited territory has everywhere been a history of more or less sustained resistance, organized from above and below, to the publicly unaccountable power of potentially violent states. Hobbesian realism should not be allowed to have the last word on the subject of state violence, if only because the mosaic of contradictory tendencies that we loosely call modernity includes striking attempts to invent and deploy non-violent methods of ensuring that the institutions of violence, such as the police and the army, become publicly accountable, and therefore disembodied or 'empty' spaces of power that can be made by citizens to change their ways, precisely because they are in principle neither permanently identified with nor owned by any particular individual or power group, including the government of the day. This struggle publicly to restrain the means of violence, to subject them to open public controversy and to hinder their unpopular or reckless use, can be understood as an attempted resolution of the paradox of Damocles and a contribution to guaranteeing that the threats of violence confronting civil society from the outside are kept to a minimum. This attempted democratization of the means of state violence has multiple historical roots and has relied upon a great variety of overlapping and sometimes conflicting methods of pacification, of which nevertheless two broad subgenres can be identified.

The Philadelphian Model

The first takes the form of various political-legal or constitutional experiments with alternatives to the near dominant Westphalian model of interstate power, according to which whole regions and ultimately the globe itself must perforce be divided territorially among sovereign states enjoying a monopoly of the means of violence, each state being left free to enter into irenic agreements with others, or to make war on those states it declares to be enemies. According to a succession of relatively neglected theorists stretching from Pufendorf and Althusius to Paine, Calhoun, von Seydel and Schmitt, this model of interstate power has either never actually been hegemonic or never deserved to be hegemonic. They are less interested in modern empires, a good comparative history of which has yet to be written, than in the various modern constitutional alternatives – the old Swiss Confederation that lasted from the later medieval period until 1789, the United Provinces of the Netherlands that lasted from 1579 to 1795, the German Bund that lasted from 1815 to 1866 – that have been guided by the broad aim of developing a type of suprastate government founded upon a *foedus* or treaty among states, whose rulers and ruled see the distinct advantages in the practical transcendence of an anarchic system of sovereign states prone constantly to war and threats of war. The Philadelphian model, born of the American colonists' struggle against the British and institutionalized as the United States of America between the establishment of the union (1781–89) and the Civil War (1861–65), is an example that ought to be of interest to contemporary theorists of violence since the whole point of this model is to institutionalize the means of violence in such a way that the unaccountable quality of state violence and the bellicose anarchy among states typical of the Westphalian model are overcome.[22]

The core structures of the Philadelphian model, described by James Madison as a 'compound republic', combined forms of popular (male) sovereignty exercised as citizens' rights within civil society, including the right to a free press and (twisting Hobbes's maxim that covenants without the sword are nothing) the right to bear arms, codified in the Second Amendment: 'A well-regulated Militia, being necessary to the security of a free State, the right of the people to keep and bear Arms, shall not be infringed.' The principles of the Philadelphian model also included the formal equality of the member states of the union; a balance and division of power among and within the two-tiered system of state institutions, including its policing procedures and war-making powers (symbolized, for instance, by the subdivision of powers of war-making, military command and foreign affairs between the president and a divided Congress); and, by means of this check-and-balance architecture of armed power, the maintenance of a citizens' militia as a means of restraining the central government from waging unpopular foreign wars. In sum, the model was driven by an overall desire to avoid the emergence of another Europe, which was seen to be

[22] See Gerald Stourzh, *Alexander Hamilton and the Idea of Republican Government*, Stanford, Calif. 1970; Daniel H. Deudney, 'The Philadelphian System: Sovereignty, Arms Control, and Balance of Power in the American States-Union, circa 1787–1861', *International Organization*, volume 49, number 2, Spring 1995, pp. 191–228; and my account of Thomas Paine's advocacy of federalism in the new American republic in *Tom Paine: A Political Life*, New York and London 1995, chapter 7.

racked by hierarchy, balance-of-power politics and constant wars between and among states.

Some elements of this Philadelphia model, especially the will to overcome the violent anarchy of the unregulated nation-state system by means of political-legal regulation and the public apportioning of power over the means of violence, have found their way into such twentieth-century constitutional experiments as the League of Nations, the United Nations and the European Union. They have been supplemented with supranational political-legal arrangements which attempt to criminalize certain forms of state violence. The International Military Tribunals at Nuremberg and Tokyo and, most recently, the Hague International Tribunal, are examples of pathbreaking (if heavily flawed) efforts to define and to prosecute war crimes, crimes against humanity (such as rape) and genocide. These tribunals have certainly triggered new controversies: to do with their self-establishment without legal precedent and, therefore, by means of multilateral agreements (the Tokyo tribunal, for instance, was largely controlled by the Americans); the widespread suspicion that they are kangaroo courts or even show trials dispensing victors' justice *ex post facto* (thus violating the old legal principle, *Nullum crimen sine lege; nulla poena sine lege*); new disputes about how to define unambiguously war crimes (otherwise described as 'grave breaches of international humanitarian law') and their appropriate means of punishment; and, perhaps most importantly, criticisms of the ongoing failure of 'the international community' to establish a permanent international criminal court. Notwithstanding such disputes, these war crimes tribunals have arguably begun to unpick the key assumption of

Westphalian jurisprudence, defended by political thinkers as different as Pufendorf, Vattel and Hegel, that international law ought to reflect the will of sovereign territorial states, whose self-centred nature compels them to define and to respect their international commitments only in so far as their territorial power interests are honoured. Twentieth-century war crimes tribunals have directly challenged this precept: they revive and amend the old Christian doctrine of 'just war', with its imperatives of discrimination and proportionality, and its converse principle, 'just cause', according to which violence may be used to punish the guilty party in war in the name of a universal duty of solidarity with the Christian or human communities.

The twentieth-century assault on the Westphalian model has concentrated not only on reducing the quantity and types of violence within the Hobbesian world of interstate relations. Driven by the maxim that states are increasingly bellicose the more they exercise power violently over their subjects at home, international constitutional efforts have also concentrated on the domestic pacification of states. The Council of Europe, founded in 1949 with three key objectives – pluralist democracy, commitment to the rule of law and the protection of human rights – is something of a model of this strategy, since for the first time anywhere in the world it sought to codify these objectives in the European Convention of Human Rights and to provide mechanisms for enforcing them effectively. Observance of these objectives is considered the key condition of a state's membership of the Council of Europe and, unlike most supranational organizations, admission to it is not automatic; applicant states must first accept both its Statute (which embodies the three objectives) and scrutiny of their laws and practices to establish whether in fact the objectives are being fulfilled.

The Council of Europe's role in defending individuals' rights, regardless of their formal citizenship status, goes well beyond scrutinizing individual states' laws and practices at the time of entry. Membership also entails a continuous obligation to observe these rights, which the council seeks to ensure by means of specific enforcement procedures, including the prospect of a member state, after the exhaustion of domestic remedies, being taken to the quasi-judicial European Commission and the European Court of Human Rights in Strasbourg. Among the unusual aspects of the enforcement process is that violations of human rights, such as freedom from torture, are deemed to extend to potential or actual incidents outside a state's territory (as in cases of deportation or extradition of an individual to a country where he or she is at risk of state violence). The enforcement process also tries to address the fact that even when a state is deemed to have violated a basic human right its policing and justice system may carry on as before. It does so through such mechanisms as the Torture Committee, which has the specific mandate of examining, by means of visits, the treatment of individuals deprived of their rights with a view, where necessary, to protecting them from inhuman or degrading treatment or punishment. The Torture Committee works on the assumption that state violence against its subjects flourishes when hidden from the public eye, and its overall strategy is therefore describable as the exposure of concealed violence. Although the committee must give prior notification of a visit to a particular country, that state is obliged to permit its visits unannounced to any place within the state's jurisdiction, including prisons, military barracks, asylum centres, hospitals for the mentally ill and children's homes. The Torture Committee also tries to counter the state's propensity to conceal its violence through the element of surprise, which is reflected in the limited timescales (usually two weeks) of its announced but unscheduled visits. It further relies on the tactics of interviewing allegedly violated individuals in private and alerting local pressure groups to provide additional relevant information. After each visit, the committee is required to produce a report, whose publication depends upon either the request of the state party – which is becoming the norm – or the unilateral decision of the committee to embarrass that state by making the report publicly available.

The Politics of Civility

Efforts to restrain the Westphalian model of interstate power and to democratize the means of state violence are not exclusively concentrated within the constitutional sphere. They also arise from within civil society, where they assume the quite different form of public initiatives that aim to problematize and to reduce the quantity and arbitrariness of (threatened) state violence. Whether these initiatives succeed, or to what degree, is not at issue here, for the important point to recognize is that this long century of violence has witnessed, for the first time on any scale, what might be called a *politics of civility*, that is, organized citizens' initiatives seeking to ensure that nobody 'owns' or arbitrarily uses the means of state violence against civil societies at home and/or abroad. Those like Elias who ignore this new politics of civility are usually attached, sometimes without recognizing it, to an image of the modern state first sketched by Hobbes and revived earlier this century in Carl Schmitt's sympathetic interpretation of the modern state as the 'mortal God', as the first artificial product of the modern technological world, as a humanly invented mechanism of command that leads the struggle, if necessary by means of violence, against all domestic and foreign competitor powers, actual or potential.[23] This Hobbesian view of the state is becoming unrealistic. Recent citizens' efforts to publicize and denounce the use of rape as a weapon of war, to argue the illegality of nuclear weapons in such bodies as the International Court of Justice or to block the detonation of these weapons by direct action, serve as a reminder that peace is of concern not only to statesmen, generals and diplomats, but to citizen-civilians as well.

Exemplary of this trend is the twentieth-century growth of peace movements, which have their spiritual and organizational roots in two older currents of the modern pacifist tradition: separational pacifism, whose proponents, though accepting the magistrate's sword as a necessary evil in the world, rejected participation in civil government by their own members; and the integrational pacifism evident in the civil initiatives of groups like the Quakers, who rejected not government but its use of injurious force.[24] The onset of total war and the advent of nuclear weapons in the twentieth century have arguably nurtured the growth of peace initiatives, a striking example of which is the swelling peace movement in

[23] Carl Schmitt, *Der Leviathan in der Staatslehre des Thomas Hobbes*, Hamburg 1938.

[24] Peter Brock, *Pacifism in Europe to 1914*, London 1972.

Britain during the first half of the 1980s.[25] Judged by its number of activists, supporters and sympathizers, that movement was more popular than its predecessors in the 1950s and 1960s – the early Campaign for Nuclear Disarmament and anti-Vietnam War protests – and it arguably represented one of the largest single social movements of modern European history. The movement was marked by two striking characteristics. First, it managed to bring the subject of nuclear weapons out from under a shroud of official secrecy and scientific-technical expertise into the field of active public discussion, much of it based at the level of the small group. The new peace movement invented autonomous public spheres of debate, action and disobedience in opposition to the bellicose nationalism and nuclear weapons policy of the Thatcher government, and in respect of its anti-statism it can be seen in retrospect to have constituted an important phase of the long-term struggle for renewing and enriching old British traditions: parliamentary democracy, independent public criticism, and suspicion of overextended power. The movement was marked, secondly, by a great diversity of goals and methods. Its remarkable pluralism was expressed in its highly decentralized and diverse patterns of social support; in its thousands of campaign groups, service-oriented organizations and lateral groups drawing upon particular constituencies; and in its reliance upon a bewildering variety of concrete objectives and actions, which ranged from street petitioning, pressuring local parliamentary representatives and organizing

[25] The following is a brief summary of John Keane, 'Civil Society and the Peace Movement in Britain', *Thesis Eleven*, number 8, 1984, pp. 5–22.

nuclear-free zones, to such forms of direct action as 'die-ins', the refusal to handle and transport nuclear waste and the encirclement of nuclear bases.

Given the plurality of its concrete social and political strategies and patterns of support, this peace movement, like all contemporary social movements, cannot easily be analysed and summarized in general propositions. The movement's preoccupation with the phased deployment of Cruise missiles on British and continental European soil was nevertheless a key unifying factor and a clue to understanding why the movement as a whole should be considered an important contribution to the politics of civility. It is not by chance that these weapons systems became the most visible symbols of what had to be opposed unconditionally, for these missiles were widely viewed within the movement as the most advanced expression of a strategic doctrine that developed during the 1950s, and that later became conventional wisdom among nuclear strategists, research technicians, industrial producers and political elites: the doctrine of counterforce. This doctrine asserted (in its various forms) that technical precision and the controlled and limited use of force could be introduced into the fighting of nuclear battles. It replaced, or at least supplemented, the view of the late 1940s and early 1950s that the threat of mutual assured destruction (MAD) would deter enemies and ensure the reign of universal peace; that safety, as Churchill put it, was to be the child of terror, survival the twin brother of annihilation. By early 1980, when the numbers of activists and sympathizers within the peace movement began to swell, this old doctrine of MAD had given way to a new and undoubtedly more dangerous official policy – counterforce – whose newly miniaturized and more precise arsenals were packaged in the language of 'Air-Land Battle', 'flexible response', 'surgical strikes' and (in the Soviet version) 'defence through war-fighting'. In the course of four decades, in other words, research, development and strategic deployment of weapons had moved from H-bombs and ABMs, through multiple warheads and MIRVs (multiple independently targeted warheads) to 'first strike' and 'flexible' weapons such as neutron bombs, SS20s and Cruise and Pershing.

This development of 'tactical weapons' arguably lowered the threshold separating nuclear from conventional arms. It supposed, contrary to von Clausewitz, that war, even nuclear war, could be free of friction, and therefore restricted and winnable. It was this so-called modernization of nuclear weapons policy that the movement sensed to be perilous. The process of deterrence was seen widely to be unstable, leading to preparations for a type of war that would be qualitatively different, and certainly worse, than the old European wars of Napoleon and Frederick II. The claim (defended in the early 1980s by Atlanticists and leading neoconservatives such as Roger Scruton) that the policy of deterrence had 'kept the peace since '45' was therefore rejected as an apology for what E.P. Thompson, the movement's most famous publicist, called exterminist tendencies. Détente was seen as synonymous with the steady increase of more advanced and ever more dangerous and 'decadent weapons' (Kaldor), whose level of sophistication and hypercomplexity rendered them vulnerable to mechanical and human failures. The famous 1958 warning of Bertrand Russell that some unforeseen circumstance might spark off a world-wide catastrophe was widely felt. The movement saw détente as equivalent to an incumbent prime minister who vowed publicly to press the button when pushed; to a perilous and always tottering-on-the-brink pattern of pseudo-negotiation and struggle for 'advantage' and 'superiority' between the superpowers, in which (as the failed Geneva INF and START talks indicated) negotiations and arms control agreements were at best momentary pauses within a wider process of arms proliferation and military posturing. Under pressure from détente, many within the movement believed, existence was beginning to degenerate into the state of nature described by Hobbes; there developed a sense that the constant rearmament associated with the modernization of nuclear (and chemical and biological) weapons was an endless struggle for power that could only ever end in death on a mass scale.

This was one of the key reasons why civil society in Britain began to rouse itself during this period. Large sections of the population began to lose trust in the official image of 'deterrence', which they criticized and resisted as a codeword for rearmament, as a new ideology of state power. Détente, the supposed easing of strained relations between states and citizens, had the unintended effect of producing a generalized anxiety about the visible increase in the scope and power of the nuclear state and its repertoire of new and improved weapons – like ground-launched Cruise missiles that must be fired from civilian areas, or nuclear submarines carrying Polaris and Trident missiles, each holding a pay-load 2500 times more destructive than one Hiroshima bomb. This anxiety was evident, for instance, in the widespread belief at the time that nuclear war was probable within the next decade. It was also apparent in the panicky outrage produced by the government's 'civil defence' circulars, which emphasized the need for the state to control the sick, starving and dying survivors of a nuclear attack through commissioners with dictatorial powers, armed police, special courts and internment camps; and, above all, in the mixture of laughter and fear catalysed by the 1980 Home Office pamphlet *Protect and Survive*, which brought the subject of nuclear war into the heart of civil society by instructing every household, in 'humane' language, how to survive a nuclear war by taking down its curtains, stocking up on batteries and mechanical clocks, crouching under tables and stairways, and tuning into the BBC.

Through such experiences, various groups and institutions within civil society caught a glimpse of themselves as passive hostages in a wider struggle among nuclear states. Détente began to have another unintended effect – the perceived destruction of civil society – in that it promised the permanent threat of smouldering war or total destruction by symbolically dissolving the distinction between the 'experience of the front' (in the words of the distinguished Czech philosopher, Jan Patočka) and the safe hinterland normally associated with wars prior to the early part of this century. Memories of saturation bombing and firebombing whole cities and civilian populations returned. The apocalypse of the front, in which troops struggle to endure a night of absurdity and horrible death in order to secure for others back home a life of peace, became generalized; the nightmarish experience of the front acquired a special significance for the *whole* of civil society.

By giving public form and direction to this generalized anxiety, the British peace movement generated deep support within all strata of civil society. But active repulsion against the menacing possibility of total war was not its only achievement. As its vigorous campaigns for nuclear-free zones demonstrated at the time, the movement heightened civil society's sense that its hard-won democratic freedoms were at stake. The half-baked nuclear peace, in which the antagonists mobilize in order to demobilize their opponents, was widely felt to accelerate the militarization of society and to promote the growth of the dictatorial elements deeply ingrained within the 'liberal' welfare state. The movement helped important parts of civil society conclude that there had been a violation of the contract between civil society and the state – an old theme in British political culture, according to which individual citizens intuitively grant their loyalty to the state in return for its guarantee of their personal freedom and security. This is why the reaction of civil society nurtured by the peace movement against the state was not a 'zoological' defence of mere life, the slavelike expression of the inability to fight (and to die) for freedom.[26] The movement was in other words not merely a fearful reaction against the possibility of death by nuclear battle, but *also* a resistance to intrusive and violent forms of state power that were seen potentially to restrict and overwhelm the plurality of independent associations that are the stuff of which civil society (ideally) consists.

---

[26] Cornelius Castoriadis, *Devant la guerre*, Paris 1981, volume 1.

Judging Violence

THE POTENTIAL CONTRIBUTIONS of civilian peace initiatives to the project of democratizing the means of state violence force us to rethink the standard objection that democracy tends always to degenerate into violence. Its first celebrated version appeared in the eighth book of Plato's *Republic*, where democracy is described not as the government of the people but of the poor against the rich. The principle of democracy is said to be liberty, which is quickly transformed into licence due to the lack of public and private restraint typical of democrats; such licentiousness is reinforced by the increase in superfluous needs and immodest desires, the lack of respect for law and the general tendency to question authority, so that the old condescend to the young, parents fear their children, 'the master fears and flatters his scholars and the scholars despise their masters and tutors'. Polybius repeated this later famous line of reasoning: 'For the people, having grown accustomed to feed at the expense of others and to depend for their livelihood on the property of others, as soon as they find a leader who is enterprising but is excluded from the honours of office by his penury, institute the rule of violence; and now uniting their forces massacre, banish, and plunder, until they degenerate again into perfect savages and find once more a master and monarch.'[27]

[27] Plato, *The Republic*, book 8, section 563a, in B. Jowett, ed., *The Dialogues of Plato*, New York 1897; Polybius, *The General History of Polybius*, London 1756, book 6, section 9.

Incivility and Civil Society

This conventional view of democracy as synonymous with violent struggles for power, repeated in Reinhart Koselleck's influential critique of eighteenth-century intellectuals' loss of concern with the dangers of civil war and their love affair with democratic 'Revolution',[28] is contradicted by the involvement of citizens in peace movements, which may be seen as part of a broader development during the twentieth century of a politics of civility that encompasses such diverse themes as campaigns against homicide and the rape of women, violence against children, cruelty to animals and the concealed violence of disciplinary institutions like prisons, asylums and schools. One of the ironic effects of these campaigns is to heighten the shared perception of many citizens that civil society is riddled with dangerous pockets of violence in need of avoidance or containment or treatment or repression or new social policies. In practice, this sense of the omnipresence of violence is reinforced by various factors – from the risk and safety requirements of insurance companies to government 'law and order' campaigns and citizens' willingness to report violence to the authorities – that together have the long-term effect of highlighting to the members of civil society their own propensities to violence. These various factors not only ensure that statistical 'facts' about violence are always and necessarily 'fictitious' (a point appreciated by criminologists); they also cast doubt upon Elias's claim that civilized societies forget their genealogy and take for granted as natural their own civility.

---

[28] Reinhart Koselleck, *Kritik und Krise. Eine Studie zur Pathogenese der bürgerlichen Welt*, Munich 1959.

The point can be toughened: *All known forms of civil society are plagued by endogenous sources of incivility*, so much so that one can propose the empirical-analytic thesis that incivility is a chronic feature of civil societies, one of their typical conditions, and, hence, normatively speaking, a perennial barrier to the actualization of a fully 'civilized' civil society. 'Gradually violence on the part of the existing powers will diminish and obedience to the laws will increase,' predicted Kant when reflecting on the advantages of republican government and civil society. 'There will arise in the body politic perhaps more charity and less strife in legal disputes, more reliability in keeping one's word, and so on, partly due to love of honour, partly out of well-understood self-interest.'[29] The presumed or implied positively teleological relationship between civil society and violence in this formulation is unwarranted; civil society, contrary to Kant, is not necessarily synonymous with the drift towards 'perpetual peace'. A highly developed civil society can and normally does contain within itself violent tendencies, that is patterns of incivility or behaviour prone to violence that can and do threaten to accumulate synergetically to the point where the occasional violence of some against some within a civil society degenerates into the constant violence of all against all of an uncivil society, a state-framed ensemble of social institutions that are not merely prone to but actually dominated by uncivil forms of interaction, ranging from

[29] Immanuel Kant, 'Welchen Ertrag wird der Fortschritt zum besseren dem Menschengeschlecht abwerfen?' (1798), in *Der Streit der Facultäten in drey Abschnitten*, in *Schriften zur Anthropologie, Geschichtsphilosophie, Politik und Pädagogik*, Darmstadt 1975, part 2, section 2, p. 365.

everyday rudeness tinged with veiled threats of bodily harm to systematically organized violence. Civility evaporates. There remains a battleground, in which the stronger – thanks to the survival of certain civil liberties – enjoy the licence to twist the arms of the weaker. Under extreme conditions, an uncivil society can even haemorrhage to death. Uncivil war looms.

When using the old-fashioned adjective 'uncivil', it should be clear that I am not referring to the various forms of action originally described by Henry David Thoreau's *On the Duty of Civil Disobedience* (1849) as civil disobedience, that is, vigorous acts of deliberate lawbreaking or extroverted acts of disputed legality, whose stated aim is to bring before a public either the alleged illegitimacy or ethical or political indefensibility of certain government laws or corporate or state policies.[30] So understood, civil disobedience is not synonymous with incivility, even though it is often denounced by those who fear or disapprove of it as uncivilized or lawless or violent. Thoreau himself publicly defended a decision not to pay taxes to a government which sanctioned slavery, while Mahatma Gandhi, who did more than anybody in the twentieth century to popularize the strategy of civil disobedience, helped forcibly to obstruct British imperial government; in each case, and in subsequent cases of the use of civil disobedience as a strategy of agitation for change, those who engage in acts of provocation and confrontation are deliberately committed to *nonviolence* as a means of contesting illegitimate power, for the purpose of *strengthening* civil society.

---

[30] See Heinz Kleger, 'Ziviler Ungehorsam, Zivilitätsdefizite und Zivilitätspotentiale', *Forschungsjournal neue soziale Bewegungen*, March 1994, pp. 60–69.

Within an uncivil society, by contrast, there is certainly no shortage of spaces of interaction for vigorous activities operating at a distance from state institutions. It is precisely that freedom that tends to spawn the growth of violence. But what exactly is the meaning of this much-used, much-abused term 'violence'? Like all concepts in the social sciences, categories like violence can be fatal for the imagination essentially because they provide a potentially false sense of certainty about the world; on the other hand, without such categories, thinking is wounded, sometimes fatally, and it therefore follows that a political theory of violence needs to be aware of the need for sharp-edged categories that are as necessary as they are dangerous. It is essential to recognize that the term 'violence' is notoriously contested, and that its scope and meaning change through time and from space to space: Darnton's gripping account of cat-burnings in pre-1789 France and current controversies about cruelty to animals remind us that acts that were once considered in a certain context nonviolent and carnavalesque are, at a later moment and in a different context, regarded as strangely cruel curiosities; a similar plasticity of the term is displayed in its extension from the core domains of the military and criminal law to other spaces of life and classes of action, as has happened during the past several decades with the remarkable emergence of the term 'family violence'.[31] These spatial and temporal variations serve as an unavoidable complication in theorizations of

[31] Robert Darnton, *The Great Cat Massacre and Other Episodes in French Cultural History*, Harmondsworth 1991; Wini Breines and Linda Gordon, 'The New Scholarship on Family Violence', *Signs: Journal of Women in Culture and Society*, volume 8, number 3, Spring 1983, pp. 490–531.

violence. But still I want to insist on the need to preserve its original and essential core meaning, untainted by loose metaphorical allusions (as when a standard or treaty is 'violated' or somebody is said to suffer a 'violent convulsion' or shakes 'violently' or whose speech acts are described as 'violent' because they are passionate or immoderate) or unhindered by questions of motivation (people can be violent for a bewildering variety of reasons) or legality (violence can be, and is often, not merely the unlawful exercise of physical force) or weighed down by mistaken, if commonplace, presumptions, such as the conviction that violence against things is somehow equivalent to violence against people, as if people are the same as property.

As used in these reflections on the subject, the concept of violence has old-fashioned connotations traceable to the earliest (late medieval) English usages of the term (from the Latin *violentia*) to describe 'the exercise of physical force' against someone who is thereby 'interrupted or disturbed' or 'interfered with rudely or roughly' or 'desecrated, dishonoured, profaned, or defiled'. It is important to preserve this older and more precise meaning of violence not only because of its continuing pertinence in a long century of violence, but also because attempts (such as Johan Galtung's) to stretch its meaning to include 'anything avoidable that impedes human self-realization' effectively makes a nonsense of the concept, linking it to a questionable ontological account of 'the satisfaction of human needs' and making it indistinguishable from 'misery', 'alienation', and 'repression'.[32] Violence is better understood as the

[32] Johan Galtung, *Transarmament and the Cold War: Peace Research and the Peace Movement*, Copenhagen 1988.

unwanted physical interference by groups and/or individuals with the bodies of others, which are consequently made to suffer a series of effects ranging from shock, bruises, scratches, swelling or headaches to broken bones, heart attacks, loss of limbs or even death. Violence can of course take the form of enforced self-violation (as in suicide or 'voluntary' euthanasia), and it can be consciously intended or half-unintended, the extreme cases of which are injury caused by recklessness or institutionally produced violations of individuals or whole groups. But in each case, violence is a relational act in which the object of violence is treated, involuntarily, not as a subject whose 'otherness' is recognized and respected, but rather as a mere object potentially worthy of bodily harm, or even annihilation. The stipulation that violence is *unwanted* physical interference with a subject – as when a woman has her thighs forced apart by a man who stuffs her vagina and/or anus with a revoltingly alien organ – is expressed in such sayings as 'He laid violent hands on her' or 'He was in a violent temper'. It is also manifested in cases of institutional violence, such as those analysed by Michel Foucault, in which the bodies of subjects are confined, against their will but in the name of their improvement, in houses of discipline and punishment in which, so to say, violence is redeployed from public sites of punishment, sanitized and camouflaged within the walls of the prison, hospital, asylum.

To emphasize the involuntary character of violence implies that violence is one – extreme – form of the denial of a subject's freedom to act in and upon the world. However that subjectivity and freedom are defined – narrowly liberal or property-centred or European ways of life are not presumed in this discussion – violence obstructs subjects' bodily motion. Violence is thus prima facie incompatible with the civil society rules of solidarity, liberty and equality of citizens, since those individual citizens who are violated experience interference with their bodies, which may consequently suffer damage, physically and psychically. While the imagined, historically rooted, collective identities of a civil society, geographic communities or religious groupings for instance, are damaged or annihilated when their constituent members are violated – violence destroys the mutual interdependence of the living, the dead and the unborn – violence only has this effect because ultimately it bears down on and threatens embodied individuals, who are treated as mere objects, and whose bodies are deemed worthy of a kick and a punch, or a knife, a bullet or a bomb. Those who experience violence against them find in effect that they are treated, as Aristotle put it, as 'a solitary advanced piece in a game of draughts', or (as he says elsewhere) like a wild animal 'meant to be hunted'. Aristotle's formulation of course supposed the probability of violence within both the prepolitical realm of the *oikos* and the extrapolitical 'barbarian' world beyond the *polis*. 'The world would be a curious place', he remarked, 'if it did not include some elements meant to be free, as well as some that are meant to be subject to control, and if that is its nature any attempt to establish control should be confined to the elements meant for control, and not extended to all.'[33] Contemporary political thought arguably needs to leave behind this Aristotelian distinction between the (violence-ridden) realm of necessity and the (pacified) realm

[33] Aristotle, *Politica*, book 1, chapter 2, 1253a; and book 7, chapter 2, 1324b; cf. book 7, chapter 14, 1333a–1334a.

of freedom.[34] And yet Aristotle's basic insight that violence instrumentalizes potentially speaking and interacting subjects remains compelling. Rephrased in language that he would not have properly understood: a civil society protected and supported by publicly accountable state institutions implies speaking and peacefully interacting subjects, whereas the (at least temporary) effect of violence is to render them mute objects – and often to herd them into death's lair.

It is true that the term 'violence' is riddled with nuances and ambiguities, and that the concept of violence, like all concepts within and beyond the social sciences, is *idealtypisch*, and that it therefore selectively highlights certain aspects of reality, which nowhere exist in their pure form. So long as it continues to be used, the concept of violence (*Gewalt, violence, violenza, nasilje*) will for that reason of selectivity – and the complicated ethical issues it raises – forever remain controversial. The least controversial, purest forms of violence are undoubtedly those acts which result in involuntary death (or what is called in plain speech 'violent death'). Death is the potentially ultimate consequence of violence. For each individual, death is both a terminus and a reference point on the map of life, marking out the intersection of the finite and the infinite. Death may well serve as the point from which individuals evaluate their lives unencumbered by the pressures of the world; they can reflect upon what they have or have not achieved, what they have become and what might be in store for them. In this sense, death is at the same time birth, for it is precisely in death that life reaches its apogee. There are of course lots of different ways of dying. Lucky are those who can die

[34] John Keane, *Public Life and Late Capitalism*, Cambridge 1984.

among friends or relatives, with dignity, photographed or filmed with a look of indefinable authority on their brave faces. Unlucky are those – there have been several hundred million during the twentieth century alone – who are robbed of an 'individual death' (Rainer Maria Rilke), whose deaths are forced, anonymous, as if their own deaths die a sudden death, stealing from them the possibility of taking stock of their lives, past, present and future. There are as well lots of different ways of being killed, but only one result: you are dead, you are no more, you are no longer to be found anywhere. For someone, somewhere, you may become a statistic; if you are lucky, your photograph and treasured belongings will be held in perpetuity by relatives, friends, colleagues or lovers. But the truth is that those who suffer violent death have been pushed over the edge. Death is their centre of gravity. It marks the end of their fall. They are no longer on the streets, they are no longer on the food ration lists. They are not in the water and bread queues, nor in their beds, kitchens, or the arms of their loved ones. They are just blood-stained bodies covered in ants or flies, shallow graves dug in parks or the practice grounds of sports stadiums, twisted heaps in the desert, motionless hulks on stone slabs. End of story.

Pacifism?

So we come to a preliminary working ethical maxim: involuntary death by violence is a scandalous violation of the ground rules of any civil society, especially one that enjoys a maximum of democratic freedoms and equalizing solidarities. Violence and civil society cannot peacefully coexist, this maxim implies; if violence begins to plague the subjects of any civil society then that ensemble of non-state institutions passes over into the category of an *uncivil society*. But – the caveat is crucial – there exist forms of violation of the body of individuals – what I shall call *civil violence* – that are to be considered as basic, if paradoxical, conditions of the attainment or preservation of civility, at least under certain circumstances. This paradox of civil violence can be expressed at either the individual or the collective level, as the following illustrations in turn help to demonstrate.

Although the will to live is usually a brave act of defiance against the violence of captors who would like nothing better than their captives' suicide – as in the annihilation camps of the Gulag – there are sometimes circumstances in which there is no shortage of good reasons to kill oneself, and in which, thus, the act of suicide is not unreasonable. Jan Palach's brave burning of himself in Wenceslas Square in Prague in January 1969, shortly after the Russian invasion of Czechoslovakia, and his appeal, issued from his hospital bed as he lay dying, that others resist the invasion peacefully in various ways,[35] is a dramatic example of an individual act of self-violation, in which the violated subject is *forced* to choose whether to lose everything, spiritually speaking, or take his or her life both as a protest against incivility and as an expression of the wish that there be a future world freed from the scourge of violence. Driven by the conviction that everything had capsized and was drowning in nothingness, Palach's act of putting himself to death in public casts doubt upon the old prejudice that those who kill themselves, even if

[35] See the interview with Jan Kavan in Michael Randle, *People Power: The Building of a New European Home*, Stroud 1991, p. 153.

they do so spectacularly, depart from the realm of the visible and enter a zone of 'malign opacity' (Baudelaire) in which relations with others are forever destroyed. Suicide is not always a synonym for clandestinity; it can in fact be a public affirmation of civility, in which, paradoxically, the courage and principles of the person who has committed suicide ensure that she or he is lifted out of time and honoured by others with a form of immortality.

Questions concerning the definition of violence and the ethics of its use within a civil society are undoubtedly troubled by the problem of whether threatened violence against an individual can or should in certain circumstances be stopped by an individual act of violence – there is certainly a strong moral and legal case to be made for so-called foreseen permissible killing in bodily self-defence[36] – and the problem of whether individuals' choice to suicide, strictly speaking, is anything like a self-chosen act, or whether it is better understood as a desperate act of last resort when the subject perceives that most or all other options have been taken away, and that this remains as the most civil way of completing one's existence on earth. Steeped in the customs and conventions of the civilizing process and encouraged by modern advances in medicine, we moderns blanch at such questions, despite the ironic fact that Christianity, which refuses to sanction suicide, is founded on an act of self-sacrifice (John Donne even contended that Jesus

---

[36] The ethical and legal issue of whether individuals have a positive right of self-defence and, if so, whether and in which ways there ought to be limits upon the exercise of this right, is explored in Suzanne Uniacke, *Permissible Killing. The Self-Defence Justification of Homicide*, Cambridge and New York 1994.

committed suicide); and despite the bitter pill that some honest liberals have been forced to swallow: that the principle of self-determination of the citizen implies and requires the principle of self-destruction. Many of us prefer to regard death as the potentially avoidable entropy of the body, as the last great barrier to immortality. The age of pestilence and famine seems to be behind us; so long as we are lucky to avoid a brush with fatal accidents or grossly uncivil acts, death for around 80 per cent of citizens in the developed world has been transformed into a more or less distant destination at the end of a long, winding and predictably downhill road called delayed degenerative disease.[37] Death loses its sting, but so too does the perfectly worded suicide note of Charlotte Perkins Gilman: 'I have preferred chloroform to cancer.' Suicide seems irrational. Although the corpses of those who take their own lives are no longer dragged, beaten and mutilated, through the streets by a braying crowd who gather to watch and taunt their ignominious burial alongside a lonely stretch of highway, those who suicide still incur the prejudice of clinicians who think them manic or depressive, moralizing clergy who judge them evil, and life insurance agents who look unfavourably on their heirs, sometimes frustrating their inheritances. Few seem to understand that, under circumstances that are already given, death can be rationally chosen, that suicide can serve to affirm a life well-lived before the deterioration of the body sets in, bringing with it physical or emotional damage that appears to the subject as worse than death itself. That at least is the

[37] A good survey of the history and changing attitudes towards death by suicide is Margaret Pabst Battin's *Ethical Issues in Suicide*, Englewood Cliffs, N.J. 1995.

case of those who champion physician-assisted death or voluntary euthanasia in circumstances of terminal illness. Still fewer seem to understand Jan Palach's personal conviction that a noble death is always preferable to an ignoble life. Under despotic conditions, suicide is of course a consciously willed but not freely chosen decision. Those like Palach who end their lives would likely not do so in the absence of a conquering power. Yet in those contexts, suicide arguably serves to distinguish a citizen from a subject. As Shakespeare's Antony pointed out, suicide sends a clear message to friends and foes alike: 'I am conqueror of myself.'

Any consideration of the ethics of violence must also confront the possibility, whether intended or not, that there are times and places when the deployment of violence by whole groups against their opponents may serve as a basic condition of building or developing a civil society marked by tolerance, pluralism and democratic procedures. It has often been said that those who take up the sword shall perish by the sword. 'Blessed are the meek, for they shall inherit the earth. . . . Blessed are they which are persecuted for righteousness' sake, for theirs is the Kingdom of Heaven,' others add. But, as Simone Weil pointed out, there are times when the meek defenders of civil society, those who refuse to take up the sword, or relinquish it, simply perish on the cross after suffering indescribable hell on earth. That is why the collective deployment of violence against others may sometimes serve, against all odds, as a symbolic moral protest against absolute evil and, therefore, as a signal to future generations that gross incivility will not be tolerated. The Warsaw ghetto uprising against Nazi occupation, or the tactic of Auschwitz prisoners responsible for washing and ironing SS uniforms to search for comrades who had died of typhus, pick the racially unprejudiced lice off their corpses and slip them under the collars of the neatly ironed military jackets of their future victims, are examples. Collective violence may also serve effectively to stop the perpetrators of violence in their tracks, throwing them off balance, causing them to panic, to act confusedly, even to lay down their arms or to abandon the conflict, as in the British resistance to Nazism during World War II and in some successfully executed 'wars of liberation', such as that waged in Eritrea against the Ethiopian regimes of Haile Selassie and Colonel Mengistu. Finally, collective violence may have a profoundly transformative effect upon individuals, enabling them to shake off fear and servitude and to live as citizens. It is questionable whether the exercise of violence can always have a liberating cathartic impact upon the violent individual, as for instance Fanon's call for revolutionary violence of the colonized against the colonizers supposed. Fanon's account (in *Peau noire, masques blancs* [1952] and *Les Damnés de la terre* [1961]) of how the depersonalized colonial subject can violently defeat the system of violence that dislocates and disempowers it not only romanticizes the gun and the bomb, but does so by investing the tactic of violence with a hotchpotch faith in existentialist humanism, a crudely modernist belief in history as progress towards perfection and a sociodiagnostic psychiatry that together explained away the scraps of evidence within his own clinical reports of individuals deeply disturbed by the agitated hallucinations and terrifying phantoms caused by their own violent acts of 'liberation'. And yet – the qualification is vital – there is plenty of modern evidence that there are times and places when acts of collective violence serve to lift the spirits of the unjustly treated, to give them the courage to stand against those who violate them and even eventually to triumph without proceeding to massacre their conquered opponents.

The American Revolution is something of a prototype of this modern form of collective resistance backed by force of arms. It is true that, unlike the total wars that followed the French Revolution, the American struggle for independence was a part-time war in which the struggle for territory and military superiority was subordinated to the battle for the hearts and minds of the population. The war allowed time off from battle, and that is why, even when the American forces were unsure of survival, let alone victory, they found time to recuperate from their duties without immediate fear of being dragged away by their British enemies. It is also true that, compared with most modern revolutions, the American upheaval witnessed comparatively limited use of physical violence and intimidation, even as a threat. The general tactic of smoking out loyalists from the nooks and crannies of civil society by means of purgative rituals such as taking and publishing names, oath taking and threats to confiscate property was widely practised at the local community level, and with considerable success.[38] The tactic of rendering suspected loyalists social outcasts was designed to avoid violence and counter-violence. It effectively confronted loyalists with two choices: conform or leave. No more than one loyalist in eight left the United States, but many more chose to switch localities, most of them unharmed by violence.

The Americans' struggle against the British Empire

[38] John W. Shy, 'Force, Order, and Democracy in the American Revolution', in *The American Revolution: Its Character and Limits*, Jack P. Greene, ed., New York and London 1987, pp. 78–9.

nevertheless relied crucially at certain moments on the use of violence to crush their enemy's will to power and to build a new federated republic. The point that violence could be used for certain strictly defined ends was certainly understood by the underdressed and dispirited American troops preparing for battle at the end of 1776 against the superior forces of the British and Hessian army at Trenton, New Jersey.[39] The battle has since become part of the official American memory of the Revolution, in no small measure because at the time each side grasped, with immense seriousness, that a British victory might well cause the Americans' struggle to collapse. The Americans, for their part, badly needed a victory to divert the British threat to Philadelphia and inject new life into their flagging fight for independence. George Washington thus decided to meet the challenge by gathering volunteers from Philadelphia, a regiment of German immigrant units from Charles Lee's command and a further five hundred men subcommanded by Horatio Gates – about six thousand troops in all.

In the late afternoon light of Christmas Day 1776, officers assembled the American troops into small squads and read to them the text of Thomas Paine's *The American Crisis*. On the eve of battle, its opening sentences must have sounded strangely primeval to the ears of men thinking about death and injury. The words soon became famous and will always remain so until the cause of citizens' freedom is extinguished:

These are the times that try men's souls. The summer

[39] A fuller account of the background context, details and symbolic significance of the battle for Trenton is presented in my *Tom Paine*, chapter 5.

> soldier and the sunshine patriot will, in this crisis, shrink from the service of their country; but he that stands it *now*, deserves the love and thanks of man and woman. Tyranny, like hell, is not easily conquered; yet we have this consolation with us, that the harder the conflict, the more glorious the triumph.

After nightfall, through a storm of hail and sleet, the American troops were ferried in flat-bottomed boats across the Delaware. They inched towards Trenton, some of them leaving trails of blood in the snow from their bandaged or bare feet, their officers prodding them during halts to keep them from plummeting into an icy sleep from which they would never awake. By daybreak, the troops had reached the outskirts of Trenton. That day, 26 December, had been chosen because, one of Washington's aides remarked, the Hessian mercenaries occupying the town were known to 'make a great deal of Christmas in Germany' and would probably be sick from a surfeit of raucous dancing, schnapps and beer. The American gamble paid handsome dividends. Colonel Johann Gottlieb Rahl, the German commander at Trenton, was caught in his nightshirt and later mortally wounded in the heavy street fighting that erupted. By nightfall, the Hessians had been routed. A thousand men were taken prisoner, and, to the Americans' delight, nearly all the enemy stores, including fine German swords and forty hogsheads of rum, were captured. Trenton was won. The grip of the British Empire on America was loosened – for a while.

Violent events like the battle of Trenton force a reconsideration of Hannah Arendt's thesis that power and violence have nothing in common. 'Violence can destroy power; it is utterly incapable of creating it,' she writes, adding that the category of power should be reserved for peaceful associations of citizens who deliberately speak and act in concert.[40] Violence, Arendt insists, is by nature instrumental in that, like all means, it always and everywhere requires guidance and justification, which in turn presupposes a group of people thinking and acting in terms of the means-ends distinction. Arendt admits that in practice violence and power are commonly intertwined, but her purist insistence on their theoretical division and the primacy of the latter over the former easily lends itself to pacifist misinterpretation; it overlooks those cases (such as the American struggle for Trenton) in which violence and power are *positively* related; and, by no means least important, it underestimates the various ways in which the outcome of the violent confrontation of armed power groups acting in concert is often decided not only by power-boosting morale, but also by the timing, luck, ferocity and skill with which their weapons are deployed against each other. Violence can indeed destroy power relationships (as in despotisms, as Montesquieu pointed out), just as power relationships can sometimes stop violence in its tracks; but out of the barrel of a gun violence can also *create* bonds of solidarity, power relationships in Arendt's sense, where none had existed before.

Revolutionary Violence

The propensity, in certain circumstances, of violence to raise hopes, to stimulate awareness that things could be

[40] Hannah Arendt, *On Violence*, New York and London 1969, pp. 44–56.

otherwise and to galvanize actors' sense that they are all in the same boat has tempted some modern thinkers to glorify violence. Georges Sorel's *Réflexions sur la violence* (1908), the classic revolutionary syndicalist recipe for dramatically toppling the state by means of a mass social movement from below, is certainly intoxicated with the elixir of violence, to the point of opening itself up to the suspicion of blindness to the basic incompatibility between the respective organizing principles of violence (potential annihilation of others) and civil society (open tolerance of differences).[41] The political context in which *Réflexions sur la violence* was written differs greatly from our own, of course. Amidst the growing involvement of the socialist tradition in party politics, and inspired by a wave of anti-parliamentary activity throughout western Europe after the 1902 Belgian general strike, this work was driven by the expectation of a profound crisis of both parliamentary socialist politics and the capitalist system. It was intoxicated with the idea of an 'absolute revolution' of the workers' movement against private property, the state and political parties. Sorel expressed nothing but contempt for the 'democratic stupidity' of socialist party politics. The parliamentary road to socialism contributes blindly to the growing power and legitimacy of the modern state (Sorel specifically drew upon Tocqueville's account of

[41] Georges Sorel, *Réflexions sur la violence*, Paris 1908. The following quotations are my own translations from the third edition, Paris 1912, which includes 'Apologie de la violence', first published in *Matin*, 18 May 1908. Sorel's earliest sketch of a theory of syndicalist violence appears in *Insegnamenti sociali della economia contemporanea*, written in 1903, but published only in 1906, pp. 53–5.

the rise of democratic despotism). By so strengthening the state machinery, parliamentary socialism contradicts its declared aim of eventually abolishing the state. Furthermore, parliamentary socialism masks the contradictory interests of labour and capital. Charmed and seduced by the pettifoggery and chicanery of electoral politics, and especially by promises of social welfare legislation enacted through the state, parliamentary socialism deepens the degeneracy which drags the bourgeoisie and the proletariat far from the path assigned them in Marx's theory. Enfeebled classes, Sorel observed, foolishly always put their trust in the protective powers of the state.

Finally, the parliamentary socialist tradition is deeply implicated in the spirit of Robespierre. Sorel argued that every (attempted) political revolution from 1789 has strengthened the repressive powers of the state. Despite good intentions, a parliamentary socialist government would likely continue and worsen this trend. There are no greater protagonists of order than victorious revolutionaries. In office – here Sorel anticipated the later argument of Roberto Michels – parliamentary socialism would institute a kind of dictatorship of politicians over their followers. A parliamentary socialist government led by figures such as Jaurès would be no different from that of other political revolutionaries, who have always pleaded 'reasons of state' – and accordingly employed repressive legal sanctions and police methods – against their enemies upon coming to power.

Sorel reasoned that these disastrous political outcomes could be prevented only if the socialist movement relied upon the resolute class separatism of the proletariat. Its refusal of centralized political leadership, its native sympathy with violent action and its growing belief in the efficacy of strikes exposes the fraudulence of ruling-class attempts to mediate state and civil society through parliamentary politics. The violent direct action of the proletariat sharply polarizes civil society, which comes to resemble a field of battle between two antagonistic armies. 'The strike is a phenomenon of war.' Proletarian violence, seen by Sorel as 'beautiful and very heroic', has civilizing effects. It is the means of salvation from bourgeois barbarism. The new middle class of salaried bureaucrats crumbles, capitalist employers are forced back into their class role and class divisions are deepened and sharpened just when they seemed in danger of rotting in the marsh of parliamentary politics. Proletarian direct action, which originates in the small-scale, face-to-face *sociétés de résistance* of the trade unions, exposes and undermines the force organized by the bourgeoisie in the property and state systems. It also snaps the bonds of bourgeois habit and cowardice, and produces a new culture of solidarity in civil society. No longer blinded by party politics, the proletariat is ever more guided and inspired by myth – Sorel here drew upon Bergson – by learned bodies of shared, emotionally charged mental pictures (such as the idea of a general strike) which sharpen its determination to work towards a socialist future. The proletariat, initially in but not of civil society, ceases to be acted upon. It becomes a living social movement in possession of itself, and therefore capable of directing itself against the power of capital and its state apparatus – without the mediation of the party form or the party system. This process crystallizes in the actual drama of the general strike, likened by Sorel to a Napoleonic battle which crushes its adversary outright. The general strike of workers makes it clear, Sorel concluded, that only two historical options remain open to the socialist movement: either bourgeois decadence or the violent revolutionary struggles of the proletariat to seize productive property from private capital and thereby (note Sorel's reductionism) to abolish the state.

Parallels have sometimes been drawn between Sorel's revolutionary syndicalism and the strategy of anti-party politics that developed in central-eastern Europe between the Prague Spring and the revolutions of 1989. It is true that, notwithstanding their wholly different vocabularies, the protagonists of anti-party politics did share with the Sorelian strategy a deep antipathy to party politics and state power. But there the parallel ended, for reasons that are not only of interest to contemporary theorizations of violence but also illustrative of a certain developing suspicion of violence within the twentieth-century democratic tradition.

To begin with, most public defenders of the strategy of anti-party politics (representatives of groups such as Solidarność and Charta 77) were deeply suspicious of ideological myths. They rejected the Sorelian assumption that a single revolutionary class, arising out of the heart of civil society, could ever embody *la volonté générale*. Anti-party politics, stated simply, was a pluralistic and not a monistic type of opposition, which is also why – again in contrast to Sorel – it rejected the myth of the abolition or withering away of the state. A democratic civil society, one containing many and often conflicting elements and therefore subject constantly to controversy, innovation, the unknown and the unintended, was seen to require a framework of state institutions, which can help prevent the outbreak of serious domestic conflict as well as negotiate with other states in the international arena. Hence, anti-party politics aimed not to abolish political power, but to socialize some portion of it in order to prevent its encroachment upon matters which were considered, simply speaking, none of its business.

The democratic opposition to Soviet-type, one-party systems also rejected Sorelian-type myths of brave and heroic violence. Sorel had supposed that the nature of violence was to serve as a means for the realization of an end. 'Proletarian acts of violence . . . are purely and simply acts of war,' he wrote. 'Everything in war is carried on without hatred and without the spirit of revenge: in war the vanquished are not killed; non-combatants are not made to bear the consequences of the disappointments which armies may have experienced on the battlefield.'[42] The opponents of Soviet-style totalitarianism rejected this line of argument as dangerous. 'Taught by history', wrote Adam Michnik, 'we suspect that by using force to storm the Bastilles of old we shall unwittingly build new ones.' He continued, 'The experience of being corrupted by terror must be implanted upon the consciousness of everyone who belongs to a freedom movement. Otherwise, as Simone Weil wrote, freedom will again become a refugee from the camp of the victors.'[43] Living under a heavily armed regime which ensured that surveillance, military parades, prison and fears of violence were everyday companions of the whole population, the democratic oppositions understandably developed a deep antipathy towards the deployment of violence.[44] They consequently associated

[42] *Réflexions sur la violence*, p. 161.

[43] Adam Michnik, 'Letter from the Gdansk Prison', *The New York Review of Books*, 18 July 1985, p. 44.

[44] This experience was expressed sharply during this period in a well-known Polish anecdote, dating back to the early 1950s when sections of Polish industry were restructured to produce arms. A father badly needed a pram for his newborn child.

bravery not with heroic acts of violence (such as terrorism, assassinations or kidnappings) against their perceived enemies, but with the civilized patience of citizens who seek to live decently in an indecent regime and therefore remain unmoved by acts of violence directed against them. Writers such as Michnik saw an inner connection between violence and politics, and therefore they rejected the view that 'violence is the midwife of every old society pregnant with a new one' (Marx). Violence was seen to be the enemy of all societies, old and new. Again in contrast to Sorel, the democratic oppositions developed a fundamentally different sense of time. They rejected fantasies of apocalyptic revolution because they sensed that a precondition of a democratic civil society is that citizens acquire a measure of patience. They envisaged a peaceful transformation of the one-party system by means of a *slowly ripening* development of civil society underneath the edifice of state power.

Finally, during the period before 1989, the defenders of anti-party politics shunned violence because they sensed that the possibility of a civil society and a political democracy depends upon shaking off the presence of the one-party system within each and every individual by altering the relations of power closest to them. Those

---

Unable to find one anywhere in the shops of Warsaw, he approached a friend, who happened to be working in a factory which manufactured prams – or so he thought. This friend promised to fetch him a pram, piece by piece. Each day, the pram factory worker brought his friend bits and pieces, carefully smuggled out of the factory by stuffing them into his heavy winter overcoat. A fortnight later, the two friends decided that they now had a complete set of parts. But, the anecdote ran, when they came to assemble the bits and pieces they found that they had actually built a machine-gun.

who lived a life of anti-party politics rejected the innocent fiction that power in the one-party system was a thing to be grasped or abolished. Power was not seen to be concentrated in a single place (for example, in the upper echelons of the Party or, in Sorel's version, within the ruling class). The ruling regime was not divided between those who had power and those who were powerless. The one-party system was rather viewed as omnipresent, as a labyrinth of control, repression, fear and self-censorship which swallowed up everyone within it, at the very least by pushing them into 'voluntary servitude' (la Boétie), rendering them silent, stultified and marked by some of the undesirable prejudices of the powerful. Since the lines of power organized by the one-party system were seen to pass through all its subjects, the latter could defend themselves against it only by being different in the most radical sense, that is, by driving the system and its violence out of their own personal lives. Democratic opposition was seen for this reason to be most effective when it kept its distance from politics. Democratization was considered not merely a matter, say, of replacing party-appointed officials with a government or head of state elected once every few years. Democratization rather depended on successfully cultivating nonviolent mechanisms of self-protection, individuation and social cooperation in areas of life 'underneath' the party-dominated state: in the household, among friends, in the publishing initiative, the workplace, the parallel economy and in the sphere of unofficial culture.

The principled commitment of the democratic opposition in central-eastern Europe to the strategy of nonviolence highlights the advantages of pacifist strategies, at least under certain conditions. To begin with, principled pacifism, in so far as it adds to the plurality of forms of life on which civil societies thrive, is certainly a legitimate option that can be exercised by subjects living within a state-protected civil society haunted by violence. Pacifism adds to citizens' sense that their world is complex, heterogeneous, dynamic and therefore open to forces of contingency. Pacifism also sometimes operates as a utopia, signalling to the present or future citizens of any civil society that a world in which there is *less* violence is thinkable, perhaps even achievable. The potency of this utopia is always reinforced when peaceful but bold actions win out in circumstances seemingly hostile to the pacifist option. Not only does nonviolent collective action often nurture individuals' capacity to overcome their fears and strengthen their courage to act creatively and cooperatively.[45] There are also times when nonviolent protest literally alarms violent power. The dramatic success of Greenpeace in preventing Shell UK Limited from dumping the Brent Spar oil platform in the North Sea in the summer of 1995 is an inspiring example of collective action of this kind; so also is the brave action of Aung San Suu Kyi, who defied a cordon of heavily armed Burmese soldiers by walking slowly towards them, silently daring them to disobey orders – shouted three times – to open fire on her, forcing them to look away in disgrace, lower their rifles and allow her to pass gracefully through the cordon, flanked by her stunned

[45] Ample evidence of these effects of nonviolent public action is cited in Gene Sharp, *The Politics of Nonviolent Action*, Boston 1973; and Frederic Solomon and Jacob R. Fishman, 'The Psychosocial Meaning of Nonviolence in Student Civil Rights Activities', *Psychiatry*, volume 25, 1964, pp. 227–36.

supporters. Then there is the point, fundamentally important for a democratic theory of civil society and the state, that pacifism correctly recognizes that violence is the scourge of a democratically organized civil society simply because violence is the intended or half-intended physical denial of the existence of an individual or group of (potential) citizens. Finally, pacifism serves as a basic reminder that violence can and often does beget violence, that violence is a wild horse and that those who ride it can end up on the ground, badly hurt and dragging others in their train.

Judging Violence

The very fact that the violent are often themselves violated, such that violence kills off the potential citizen in both the violator and the violated, is often downplayed by the intellectual critics of pacifism, who instead point out, correctly in my view, that the unswerving commitment to an ultimate end grounded in a First Principle, of which principled (as distinct from tactical) pacifism is an example, often produces philosophical and political muddles, and as such is incompatible with the democratic scepticism of the state–civil society perspective. Put differently, pacifism, the explicit and principled renunciation of the use of violence even in the face of violence, is susceptible to self-contradictory dogmatism. This is especially true in circumstances in which the renunciation of violence, or the hesitation to use it, results in the tragic annihilation of the eventual victims of violence, and also in which the actual or even threatened use of counterviolence might have had demonstrably pacifying effects, convincing the aggressor to take the finger off the trigger or even to lay down arms and to live and let live. Hence Max Weber's remark: 'No ethics in the world can sidestep the fact that in many instances the attainment of "good" ends is bound to the fact that one must be willing to pay the price of using morally dubious means or at least dangerous ones – and facing the possibility or even the probability of evil ramifications.'[46]

Given the potentially unpredictable ('good' and 'bad') consequences of the decision to use or not to use violence for certain defined ends, a contemporary political theory of violence is well advised to reject both pacifism and the fetish of violence. Both indulge the same philosophical, strategic and tactical absolutism, and both therefore cloud and dangerously confuse an already complex ethico-political issue, even potentially *increasing* the probability of violence in human affairs. Political thinking should reject all talk of the need for a General Theory of the Ethics of Violence based on formal principles and abstract reasoning. It is of course true that the rejection of such talk does not resolve anything except the need to be aware of what is to be avoided. It is also obvious that the same rejection is unlikely to silence either those for whom violence is by definition anathema or those who love violence and for whom in certain contexts, like revolutions or social decay, it is an absolutely indispensable means or even a thrilling end in itself. There are people – crude-minded anarchosyndicalists, fanatical advocates of a version of *jihad* not sanctioned by the Qur'an, deranged members of millenarian cults, murderous street thugs, for

---

46 Max Weber, 'Politik als Beruf', in *Gesammelte Politische Schriften*, Johannes Winckelmann, ed., Tübingen 1958, p. 540.

instance – who believe in and/or practise that principled fetish of violence, and who therefore, if they think about it at all, normally consider what they are doing to be universal in the sense that it is absolutely true and applicable to each and every conceivable context. Since they suffer from a form of face-value thinking that absolutizes violence, they are unlikely to be persuaded by talk of pluralism and civil society. They simply want to kill. Ultimately, if democracy is to be preserved or built in their presence, they will have to be arrested or, if they resist arrest violently, dealt with by violence.

In such a case, of course, principled or unprincipled advocates of absolute violence would be ensnared in a performative contradiction. By practising their absolutist principle of violence they would bring their particular world to an end. That same outcome in ultra-Hobbesian form would also result if nearly everybody else in the world accepted their version of 'reality': the universal practice of the absolutist principle of universal violence, nuclear weapons and all, would bring their and our worlds to an end within minutes if it were strictly applied. Of course, the fanatics of violence, for instance Timothy McVeigh (chief suspect in the 1995 Oklahoma City bombing) or a suicide bomber like Bilal Fahs, one of the first Lebanese 'martyrs', might accept that outcome, and would do so with reference to some type of transcendental standard that effectively treats violence as both a means and an end; they are only able to plan the massacre of innocents or strap explosives to their bodies and go out to die along with their enemies in so far as they regard their actions as a sacramental act or divine duty executed in accordance with some theological demand or secular imperative. But if, in a moment of weakness, the fanatics of violence were to engage the argument, and face up to the absurd possibility that their commitment to violence would, when universalized by friends and foes alike, destroy everybody and everything, including themselves; and if they went on to admit that in a world of appearances, in which means and ends are contextually produced and susceptible of being seen as contingent and therefore mutable, violence is merely one valuable means or end among many others, they would perforce be confronted with the embarrassing need to recognize that their dogma of violent martyrdom is unacceptable to others, and that they would be required, if only to preserve their own physical existence, to compromise, which would imply accepting that the pricipled commitment to violence cannot and should not be universalized and that even the use of violence as a means to a designated end is necessarily subject to the potentially restrictive framework of means-ends calculations.

This implication can be clarified by considering in a fresh way the vexed relationship between the idea of a civil society and the use of violence. From the perspective of political thinking that does not rest upon foundationalist First Principles like pacifism or the fetish of violence, but instead sees the institutions of civil society and protective constitutional arrangements as necessary preconditions and outcomes of ethical pluralism, there is an elective affinity – but not an absolute bond – between nonviolence and civil society. Seen in this way, violence can be deemed 'good' only when it effectively serves as a means of the creation or strengthening of a pluralistic, nonviolent civil society secured by publicly accountable political-legal institutions, that is, when violence serves to *reduce* or to *eradicate* violence. Conversely violence, considered as a means to a designated end, can be considered 'bad' in so far as it both contradicts that end, gets out of control or results in growing quantities of violence within the specific social context or wider body politic in which it is used. This postfoundationalist reasoning of course still begs the question of whether or not violence is legitimate under democratic conditions, that is, whether there are times and contexts when it is justified to use violence for particular purposes and against one's designated opponents. This question can only be answered tentatively and by means of decisions that are formulated and applied within the unique conditions of specific temporal and spatial contexts.

This does not mean that anything goes, or that the practical use of violence and considerations about the ethics of violence are subject to the laws of blindness and arbitrariness. Normatively speaking, the decision to use or to refrain from using violence is a matter of *judgement* in the philosophical sense. Judgement, the publicly learned capacity to choose courses of action in public contexts riddled with complexity, is the democratic art par excellence. It relies neither on the rules of deduction and induction nor on the conjectural thinking of abduction. Judgement avoids flights of fancy as much as it shuns practical reason, which 'reasons' by telling actors what to do and what not to do by laying down the law in the language of imperatives like 'Thou shalt not kill' or 'An eye for an eye'. Judgement avoids categorical imperatives that instruct those who act always to act in such a way that the criteria of their acts can become a general law. Judgement tacks between the unique and the general. It is neither 'reflective' nor 'determinant' (to use the highly questionable distinction drawn by Kant to describe decisions that derive general rules from the particular or derive the particular from the general, respectively[47]). Judgement instead relies on the recognition that the practical choice of how to act in any context must be guided by the recognition of the *particularity* of that situation, which means giving recognition to its uniqueness or difference from what we are used to, and therefore to the need to compare and contrast it with previous or contemporaneous situations that more or less resemble the particular situation at hand.

Indeed, that very necessity of recognizing that we know that we do not know what is to be done, that decisions require judgements and that judgements lie within the field of force between the particular and the general are quintessential features of the art of judgement that rescue it from mere arbitrariness. In matters of violence, we can say, the most plausible working maxim is: the decision to use or not to use violence for power-political ends, whether in the household or on the battlefield, is always risky, and plagued by ongoing confusion and unintended consequences, some of which sometimes quite unpredictably contradict the stated purpose for which violence was considered the appropriate or effective means. Judgements about the utility and ethics of violence are therefore necessary. In matters of violence, to be sure, defenders of a civil society must recognize that violence normally – but not always – contradicts and erodes civility. But before giving recognition to this precept, they must recognize that the most dangerous thing confronting citizens is not that they

[47] The distinction between *die reflektierende Urteilskraft* and *die bestimmende Urteilskraft* is developed in Immanuel Kant's introduction to *Kritik der Urteilskraft*, in *Werkausgabe*, Wilhelm Weischedel, ed., Frankfurt am Main 1974, volume 10, section 5.

will violate or be violated, or kill or be killed, but rather their abstention from making judgements about violence by surrendering blindly or sheepishly to the prevailing means of violence and relationships of armed or potentially armable power. In matters of violence, as both Mahatma Gandhi and Georg Elser understood, those who flow with the tide risk ending up on the rocks of the devils' islands.

There is evidence that the delicate process of context-bound judging about violence described here is of concern not only to political philosophers but also to citizens who practise judgement calls within actually existing civil societies, as has been demonstrated in a study by Janie Ward of everyday conceptions of violence among American adolescents of mixed ethnic background.[48] A majority of respondents in this sample had themselves suffered or witnessed violence within the household or neighbourhood, and, not surprisingly, most displayed a sophisticated capacity to reason morally about the subject. A minority of respondents, those with a reflective understanding of 'care' as the basic principle needed to resolve conflicts in human relationships, typically found violence intrinsically wrong. They reasoned that violence hurt people and was 'unnecessary, since it could have been avoided through dialogue'. When pressed to assess the ethics of the actions of people who felt that they had no other means than violence to protect themselves and others from danger, the same respondents considered violence understandable, but morally wrong. A majority of respondents, by contrast,

---

[48] Janie Victoria Ward, 'Urban Adolescents' Conceptions of Violence', in Carol Gilligan et al., eds, *Mapping the Moral Domain*, Cambridge, Mass. 1988, pp. 175–200.

judged that judgements about violence were necessary and that violence was therefore justifiable within certain circumstances. Ward distinguished three different but related types of moral judgement exercised by her respondents. Those who thought in terms of the principle of rule- and rights-governed 'justice' considered violence appropriate when it was used to remedy or avenge undeserved punishment or unfair treatment. Those who instead combined 'care' and 'justice' criteria considered that in circumstances when a person was pushed to the limit and left with no other option, a woman using retaliatory violence to put an end to her suffering at the hands of a man, for instance, she or he was justified in resorting to violence, which was usually seen as an act of empowerment. A third group of respondents, those for whom ideas about 'justice' and 'care' were not simply combined but actually inseparable, judged violence – within certain clearly defined boundaries – to be a 'fair', 'tolerable' and 'acceptable' means of protecting the self and others from the danger of irreparable harm.

The Sword and the Qur'an

Political thinking can help reinforce this learned capacity for everyday judgements about the ethics of violence by clarifying and highlighting not only the possible benefits that violence sometimes brings in certain contexts, but also the permanent risks and ineradicable dangers of using violence, or certain forms of violence, in specific contexts. It is true that distinctions between different forms of violence and the different contexts in which violence is used should always be kept in mind. Those who forget or deny that a land-mine blast is not a Punch and Judy show and that a military battlefront in war is not a domestic quarrel should be suspected of woolly thinking. It is nevertheless true that in every context and in respect of every form of violence judgements are as necessary as they are difficult. At the end of a long century of violence, wise political thinking should be suspicious of romanticized violence and at the same time troubled by the evident conundrums associated with pacifism – no matter what the context or form of violence. For this purpose, the emphasis upon the *dilemmas* that permanently ensnare all who dare resort to the tactic of violating the bodies of others, especially in group conflict, is very useful.

A contemporary example will help clarify this point. Especially in countries in which Islam is potentially a dominant social force, Islamic politics is faced by a strategic difficulty concerning violence that I have elsewhere called *the transition-to-democracy dilemma*. Precisely because in Europe and elsewhere Islam has been demonized in recent years – in many circles, since the Iranian Revolution, the epithet 'Islamic fundamentalism' has been deployed not only to refer to the violent resistance of those Islamic groups and parties, especially the Shi'a, who strictly oppose the interventionist policies of the West in their lands, but as a catch-all term to refer to any and every Muslim – it is not generally understood that there are many Islamists who are presently attempting to combat the ideology of Islam-as-Fundamentalism by emphasizing Islam's capacity for nonviolent power sharing and, thus, its compatibility with modern democratic procedures such as periodic elections, parliamentary government and entrenched civil liberties. There are those – the Egyptian writer Ahmad Shawqui al-Fanjari and the Tunisian opposition leader Rachid Al-Ghannouchi have been among the boldest – who deduce every conceivable democratic right and duty from the Qur'an, the Traditions of the Prophet and the practice of the first four Caliphs. Fanjari, following the example of Tahtawi, the famous pioneer of cultural westernization in Egypt, says that every age adopts a different terminology to convey the concepts of democracy and freedom. What is called freedom in Europe is exactly what in Islam is called justice (*'adl*), truth (*haqq*), consultation (*shura*) and equality (*musawat*). Fanjari says 'the equivalent of freedom in Islam is kindness or mercy (*rahmah*) and that of democracy is mutual kindness (*tarahum*)'.[49] He goes on to remind his readers that in the Qur'an the Prophet is instructed to show leniency and forgiveness in the very same verse as he is ordered to consult the believers in the affairs of the community. The Prophet is reported to have said in turn that God 'has laid down consultation as a mercy for His community'. It follows from this interpretation that, contrary to the assertions of its Orientalist denigrators, Islam is indeed compatible with democracy because there is no place in it for arbitrary rule by one man or group of men. The basis of all decisions and actions of an Islamic state should not be individual whim and caprice, but the *Shari'ah* – the body of regulations drawn from the Qur'an and the Traditions. Ghannouchi adds that Islam passes another test of democracy, in that it satisfies the

[49] Ahmad Shawqui al-Fanjari, *Al-hurriyat' as-siyasiyyah fi'l Islam*, Kuwait 1973, pp. 31, 34, cited in Hamid Enayat, *Modern Islamic Political Thought*, Austin, Tex. 1988, p. 131. Rachid Al-Ghannouchi's theory of Islamic democracy is detailed in his *Public Liberties in the Islamic Political System*, forthcoming.

requirement that any government should reckon in all its decisions with the wishes of the ruled. In listing the qualities of a good believer, the Qur'an and the Traditions mention *shura* (consultation) and *ijima'* (consensus) on the same footing as compliance with God's order, saying the prayers and payment of the alms tax. It follows from this principle of legitimate power, argues Ghannouchi, that even in contexts where the application of *Shari'ah* is difficult or impossible, Muslims should work for *shura*, which implies joining with 'secular' forces in opposing corrupt and violent dictatorships everywhere.

This type of argument about the democratic potential of Islam deserves widespread attention. Both within the Islamic and Western worlds, cosmopolitan Islam, as I have called it,[50] is a potential force for civility, mutual toleration and power sharing, exactly because it challenges both the dogma that the teachings of Islam are essentially 'fundamentalist' and its insulting medieval corollary, traceable to the Christian Crusades, that Islamists are weapon-wielding power-mongers. And yet Islam can only be seen widely as a force for nonviolent power sharing if it can successfully deal with a strategic difficulty, to do with the means of violence, that can be called *the transition-to-democracy dilemma*.

Nearly a third of the world's believers in Islam live in countries in which they can never hope to become a numerical majority of the population. In those countries, India and France for example, Islamists have certain (overlapping) political options. They can turn their backs on the world around them (living apolitically as

---

[50] John Keane, 'Power-Sharing Islam?', in Azzam Tamimi, ed., *Power-Sharing Islam?*, London 1993, pp. 15–31.

pietist communities in accordance with Sayyid Qutb's instruction that there is an abyss between Islam and the world which is spanned not by a bridge enabling a meeting halfway between the two, but by one that allows for the 'godless' people of the *jahiliyya* to cross over to the 'true believers' of Islam). Muslims can also live their faith by caring little for the immediate non-Muslim 'unbeliever' society around them and instead bonding with other Muslims elsewhere in the wider world (the strategy of the Jama'at al Tabligh, the largest transnational Islamic organization in the world). Or, within their state or locale, these minority Islamists can live their faith and espouse the cause of toleration and civil and political liberties for all. If they refuse all of these nonviolent options, Islamists are likely to weaken their own sociopolitical and religious credibility, especially in the eyes of a potentially threatening and threatened non-Muslim majority concerned about 'Islamic fundamentalism'.

Within these countries, the transition-to-democracy dilemma hardly applies. Yet in countries and regions in which Islam is potentially a dominant social force, Tunisia or Algeria for instance, Islamic politics feels the pinch of the dilemma acutely. Any Islamic movement that attempts to transform a non-Islamic into an Islamic state (the latter is often vaguely defined as a political community based on the revealed law of Islam) is forced to choose, or to steer a perilous course, between two incompatibles – the ethical principles of Islam and the potentially violent ways and means of modern state power. Islamic parties that are dedicated to parliamentary democracy work on the assumption that their enemies are civil human beings, and this in turn limits their range of political tactics. They embrace public discussion, press conferences, vote getting and parliamentary numbers, rather than terrorism, street violence and dreams of a revolutionary putsch. When elected to office it follows that those Islamic parties eschew dictatorship as a means of staying in office. If voted out of office, as Rachid Ghannouchi has urged, they should then leave peacefully, to prepare for future electoral battles.

Of course an Islamic movement that remains faithful to its own principles and to these democratic procedures may never achieve governmental power. Many followers of Islam like to quote the Qur'an: 'O you who believe! stand out firmly for Allah, as witnesses to fair dealing, and let not the hatred of others towards you make you swerve to wrong and depart from justice. Be just, that is next to piety, and fear Allah. For Allah is well-acquainted with all that you do' (5; 8). Well and good. But especially in contexts where their opponents do not abide by the power-sharing rules of democracy, Islamists may find themselves outwitted, censored, beaten up, arrested, executed or forced into exile. Under such circumstances, which are today the norm for most followers of Islam, does this mean that the vision of a democratic Islamic state is a contradiction in terms and a practical impossibility? Or can an Islamic state be achieved only if Islamists are prepared to abandon the democratic method temporarily to attain power by violence in the pious hope that an Islamic government so formed will return to parliamentarism once Islam has assumed control? Needless to say, this second alternative contains tragic possibilities: a movement for democracy that resorts to despotic methods to achieve its goals will not remain a democratic movement for long. Its chosen means will devour its chosen ends. And yet – here is the painful dilemma – the first alternative, that of clinging to parliamentary democratic procedures under all circumstances, may well doom Islam to a permanent political wilderness, to *darul-harb*, a land of hostility and war against Islam.

The transition-to-democracy dilemma is real. A disturbing example of its failed resolution is contemporary Algeria: there the current brutal treatment of Islamists and the terrorization of the rest of society by the military-dominated High Committee of State, in whose first (subsequently voided) multiparty general elections in December 1991 the Front Islamique du Salut (FIS) won an absolute majority of votes, is matched by the retaliatory violence of certain Islamist factions, notably the GIA, who regard democracy as a kind of *jahiliyya* whose violent terror has to be combated, tooth and nail, with bombings, guerrilla ambushes, throat slashings. The Algerian savagery serves as a warning of the bleak consequences of attempting to dissolve the transition dilemma by guns and bombs, but it is not necessarily a cause for general despair. While by definition a dilemma is insoluble, its force can in practice be attenuated in various ways, and it is therefore to be hoped that contemporary political thinkers and actors in countries such as Egypt and Tunisia will set their imaginations loose on the problem of how to maximize the chances of securing a democratic Islamic state in contexts where its bully opponents do not play by the rules of the democratic game. Detailed recommendations would be inappropriate here, but three points bearing on the problem of making judgements about violence should be clear.

First, an Islamic party or government which comes to power and rules by terror, force and intrigue is a contradiction in terms. It is (to resort to the arguments of Ahmad Shawqui al-Fanjari and Rachid Al-Ghannouchi) anti-Islamic and therefore anti-democratic. Some Muslims like to speak of the Qur'anic principle that necessities eliminate prohibitions. It is as if they yearn to confirm René Girard's well-known thesis that religious rituals function to offload violence on to others, to keep violence *outside* the religious community. 'But if one is faced by necessity', they say, 'without wilful disobedience or transgressing due limits then is he guiltless.' But these Muslims also know that nowhere does the Qur'an sanction permanent violence or violence unstructured by a designated end; passages such as 'Allah does not wish to place you in a difficulty, but to purify you, and to complete His favour to you' (5; 6) can hardly be read as an incitement to unrestrained violence. The Qur'an is not synonymous with the sword. *Jihad*, the fight against godlessness outside or inside the believer, is always to be constrained by the avoidance of discord (*fitnah*), the granting of mercy (*rahmah*) and the imperative of justice (*'adl*).

Second, it should always be remembered that in the struggle for more democracy the methods used strongly condition the tactics and methods of its opponents. The latter are never simply given, and they should not be thought to be so. Successful transitions to democracy are always a learning process in which – several of the recent 'velvet revolutions' of central and eastern Europe are striking cases in point – opponents of democracy can sometimes be convinced to minimize their acts of sabotage and relinquish at least some of their power democratically. The point is that terror breeds fear and armed *jihad* breeds military crackdown, while peaceful democratic methods can be infectious, if only because even their opponents can see that they enable everybody to sleep peacefully in their beds at night.

Third, the political dilemma confronting contemporary Islamists who pursue the parliamentary road can be further weakened by their refusal to make a fetish of sovereign state power. For a variety of reasons we are witnessing, especially in certain regions such as the Maghreb and the Middle East, a crisis of nation-state sovereignty. Parts of that world are beginning to resemble the *form* of the medieval world, in which monarchs were forced to share power and authority with a variety of subordinate and higher powers. The trend has profound implications for the struggle for an Islamic state. It renders implausible the revolutionary strategy of seizing state power, if need be through the use of force, precisely because the 'centres' of state power are tending to become more dispersed and subject to (international) cross-pressures and, hence, are either immune from 'capture' by a single party or government, or (as in contemporary Iran) necessarily subject to the push and pull of social forces. Not only that, but in so far as 'the state' ceases to be in one place to be 'seized', the struggle by Islamists to monopolize state power is rendered less imperative. The often poorly coordinated and dispersed character of state power, whether in Egypt, Morocco or Malaysia, makes it ever more susceptible to the initiatives of social organizations and movements which mobilize traditional 'folk' Islam and cultivate its 'grass-roots' networks, above all in local mosques, clinics and schools, to practise the nonviolent art of divide-and-rule from below. In other words, Islam, the most socially conscious of world religions, can partly overcome the transition-to-democracy dilemma by concentrating the considerable sum of its energies on the nooks and crannies of civil society. There, in areas of life underneath and outside of the state, it can empower its followers by stimulating their awareness that large-scale organizations, such as transnational firms and state bureaucracies, even violent ones, ultimately rest upon the molecular networks of power of civil society – and that the strengthening and transformation of these micro-power relations necessarily affect the operations of these large-scale organizations.

Uncivil Society

THE STRATEGY OF supplementing the parliamentary road to Islam with the creation from below of an Islamic movement rooted in civil society offers not only a practical way of moderating the transition-to-democracy dilemma. It clearly presents the hope of greater dignity to people who have been pauperized materially and spiritually by violent states and forms of western or Soviet modernization: people such as the poor of the City of the Dead in Cairo, the inhabitants of the *gecekondu* of Istanbul and the young people from quarters in Algiers like Bab al-Oued, where talk is now mainly about elusive visas and emigration, and memories of friends killed on the streets by the crack of army gunfire. It is nevertheless vital to point out that civil society can never become a haven of nonviolent harmony. Those who work for a (more) civil society must recognize not only that violence is often the antithesis of civil society, but also that every known form of civil society tends to produce this same violent antithesis. This inner contradiction within the workings of civil society – that it tends to be a peaceful haven of incivility – has been obscured by the originally eighteenth-century theory of the upward spiral towards civilization and, more recently, by the strange silence about violence within the renaissance of the theory of state and civil society. But what exactly is the source of this troubling contradiction?

The most common explanation resorts to ontological considerations. 'We see even in well-governed states, where there are laws and punishments appointed for offenders,' wrote Hobbes, 'particular men travel not without their sword by their sides for their defences; neither sleep they without shutting not only their doors against fellow subjects, but also their trunks and coffers for fear of domestics.' Incivility is here treated as a primeval energy: 'the condition of Man . . . is a condition of Warre of every one against every one; in which case every one is governed by his own Reason; and there is nothing he can make use of, that may not be a help unto him, in preserving his life against his enemyes; It followeth that in such a condition, every man has a Right to every thing; even to one anothers body.'[51] Three and a half centuries later, Hobbes's reasoning about human nature still enjoys a reputation. This is partly because we have not yet shed the old bourgeois fascination with neo-Hobbesian themes – Peter Gay's compelling study has shown just how strong was this fascination during the past century[52] – and partly because the view of human nature as violent has a certain intuitive appeal, especially when 'the facts' seem to speak for themselves. What else but dastardly human nature is behind the evil acts perpetrated by government soldiers who chop off their victims' ears or genitals and force them at gunpoint to chew them before suffering execution? Surely the willingness of soldiers to force mothers at gunpoint to shoot their own terrified children through the head before an assembled crowd, only then to shoot the killers and the crowd itself, proves that we

[51] Thomas Hobbes, 'Preface to the Reader', *Philosophical Rudiments concerning Government and Society*, London 1651; and *Leviathan, or The Matter, Forme, and Power of a Common-Wealth Ecclesiastical and Civill*, London 1651, part 1, chapter 14.

[52] Peter Gay, *The Cultivation of Hatred. The Bourgeois Experience: Victoria to Freud*, London 1994.

have an inborn need to be violent? What else explains the perversely sadistic pleasure of the torturer who places a rat inside his victim, so beginning the slow process of death by cruel humiliation?

There can be no doubt that in order to understand such acts of violence it is vital to have an understanding of the character structure of the individual perpetrator, who, although he or she usually acts in concert with a wider group of perpetrators, is at some point in the act of violence alone with the victim and driven by inner instincts and thoughts. Armies or gangs alone do not kill, not even when violence is administered by war machines that physically or visually distance the violent from the violated. And yet when seeking to understand why individuals are violent it is equally clear that a distinction needs to be drawn between the two different types of microlevel or 'human nature' explanations, stretching from St Augustine to Freud, that seek to trace the causes of violence to human nature. First, there are those ahistorical ontologies that suppose that Man is essentially wicked (as in Machiavelli's claim that all men at all times are 'ungrateful, changeable, simulators and dissimulators, runaways in danger, eager for gain'[53]) and therefore have difficulty side-stepping institutionalist explanations in order to account for why and how individuals and, indeed, whole societies are from time to time pacific, sometimes for extended periods. Second, there are those accounts of human nature that admit that in the here and now human nature is perverted, or even bloodthirsty, but that it could in future, under different institutional

---

[53] Niccolò Machiavelli, *The Prince*, in *Machiavelli: The Chief Works and Others*, Alan Gilbert, trans., Durham, N.C. 1965, volume 1, p. 62.

circumstances, be diverted or made to assume a quite different, more pacific form, as in William James's proposal that the world would become a safer place if its youth were drafted into mining coal, manning ships, building skyscrapers, washing dishes and laundering clothes.[54]

In either case, the attempt to explain violence with sole reference to human nature is forced to admit the necessity of traditions of explanation of violence that make reference to institutional factors. Broadly speaking, there have been two different types of these explanatory traditions. One of them, mesolevel *regime theories*, insists that violence on a limited or extended scale derives primarily from the particular, historically specific organizing principles of the state or socioeconomic system, in other words, that violence stems from monarchy (Paine) or despotism (Montesquieu) or capitalism (Marx) or states structured by pre-capitalist values (Schumpeter) or totalitarian dictatorship (Arendt), and that violence will therefore only wither away or at least be attenuated if and when these particular regime types are replaced by republics or constitutional monarchies or the end of class struggle and the common ownership of the means of production or the renewal of active citizenship. The other type of explanation, macrolevel *geopolitical theories*, insists that the ultimate roots of violence are traceable to the permanently decentred international system of states, whose anarchic dynamism reflects the absence of genuinely global regulatory mechanisms and the dominance of a plurality of armed states that periodically draw otherwise civil citizens and states into the vortex of bellicose conflict.

---

[54] William James, 'The Moral Equivalent of War', in *Memories and Studies*, New York 1912, pp. 262–72, 290.

The geopolitical type of explanation, a version of which was championed by Elias, has already been examined above, and I shall therefore move to outline and defend a new version of the mesolevel or regimist explanation. Even if human nature were either essentially or circumstantially prone to violence, it would be necessary to explain how a particular social formation facilitated or hindered expressions of violence. This problem brings us directly back to the original issue of why civil societies tend to generate from within themselves various types of threatening violence. According to one (originally eighteenth-century) formulation, civil societies are best considered not as caught up in an upward spiral of progress, but rather (as Mirabeau put it) as only a brief apogee in an otherwise tragic '*natural* cycle from barbarism to decadence by way of civilization and wealth'.[55] The 'iron law' of cycles of violence first formulated by Mirabeau is implausible. It is premodern in inspiration, and is certainly hard to substantiate in either theoretical or empirical terms; the metaphysic of decline and renewal also has obstructive policy implications, since it implies that little or nothing can be done to stem the floods of violence that periodically sweep away the protective walls of civility that maintain peace among citizens. More plausible are those mesolevel theories that seek to account for the eruptions of violence by tracing them to the specific institutional structures of civil society. Here another important distinction should be drawn: between *capitalism-centred* explanations and more comprehensive *civil society-centred* explanations.

The most influential example of the former is Marx's

---

[55] Honoré-Gabriel Riqueti, Comte de Mirabeau, *L'Ami des hommes ou Traité de la population*, Paris 1756, p. 176.

emphasis on the conflict potential of the wage-labour/capital relationship. The modern bourgeois era, Marx pointed out, is unique in so far as it effects a separation of the political and social forms of stratification. It subdivides the human species for the first time into social classes; divorces individuals' legal status from their socioeconomic role within civil society (*bürgerliche Gesellschaft*); and sunders each individual into private egoist and public-spirited citizen. By contrast, feudal society had a directly political character. The main elements of civil life (property, the household, forms of labour) assumed the forms of landlordism, estates and corporations. The individual members of feudal society enjoyed no private sphere; their fate was bound up inextricably with the network of interlocking public organizations to which they belonged. The 'throwing off of the political yoke' is a distinguishing mark of modern bourgeois orders. Civil society, the realm of private needs and interests, waged labour and private right, is emancipated from political control, and becomes the basis and presupposition of the modern state.

Civil society is represented by Marx – correctly – as a contingent historical phenomenon, and not as a naturally given state of affairs. Modern, state-guaranteed civil societies do not conform to eternal laws of nature, and they certainly do not arise from their members' propensity for society. They are historically determinate entities, characterized by particular forms and relations of production, class divisions and struggles, and protected for a time by corresponding political-legal mechanisms. Not only are bourgeois civil societies products of modern times. Their life expectancy is limited inasmuch as they give birth to the proletariat, the class with radical chains, the class in civil society that is not of civil society, the potentially universal class that signals the dissolution of all classes, if need be through violence. Although he was not alone in this conviction, Marx was right to pinpoint the wage-labour/capital relationship as a potential point of violent antagonism within modern civil societies. The Marxian theses on civil society are nevertheless riddled with problems,[56] among which are Marx's mistaken assumptions that lumpenproletarian and proletarian mugging and murder would give way to the organized militancy of the working class, and his poor grasp of both the violence-producing and shock-absorbing potential of *nonmarket* institutions within civil society.

In well-established civil societies, certainly, there is comparatively limited scope for the display of strong feelings or strong antipathies towards people, let alone heated anger, wild hatred or the urge to belt someone over the head. Wherever stress-induced tensions develop, they tend to be absorbed or sublimated into the social structures, and civility prevails, or so Elias argues: 'Most human societies, as far as one can see, develop some counter-measures against stress-tensions they themselves generate. In the case of societies at a relatively late level of civilization, that is with relatively stable, even and temperate restraints all round and with strong sublimatory demands, one can usually observe a considerable variety of leisure activities with that function, of which sport is one.'[57] If that is so, then the fundamental question

---

[56] John Keane, *Democracy and Civil Society. On the Predicaments of European Socialism, the Prospects for Democracy, and the Problem of Controlling Social and Political Power*, London and New York 1988, pp. 57–64, 215–28.

[57] Norbert Elias, 'Introduction', in Norbert Elias and Eric Dunning, *Quest for Excitement. Sport and Leisure in the Civilizing Process*, Oxford and Cambridge, Mass. 1993, p. 41.

remains unanswered: Why do the shock-absorbing institutions of civil societies tend to be overburdened, such that they generate from within their own structures patterns of violence that contradict the freedom, solidarity and civility which otherwise make them so attractive?

The openness that is characteristic of all civil societies – their nurturing of a plurality of forms of life that are themselves experienced as contingent – is arguably at the root of their tendency to violence. The well-recognized fact that they enable groups to organize for the pursuit of wealth and power, for instance, has made their capitalist economies not only restlessly dynamic at home, but also prone to expansion on a global scale, one consequence of which has been the widespread exporting of violence to tribes, regions, nations and whole civilizations considered rude or savage. Modern civil societies have provided handsome opportunities for certain power groups tempted by dreams of expansionism, and this has ensured that the whole modern history of colonization and bullying of the uncivilized has been riddled with violence, to the point where it may be said, with a touch of bitter irony, that the current worldwide appeal of civil society is the bastard child of the violence of metropolitan civility.

The legal or informal freedom to associate in complex ways that is afforded the members of any civil society also makes them prone to violence at home. There are several reasons for this. One of them has to do with the fact that civil societies, ideal-typically conceived, are complex and dynamic webs of social institutions in which the opacity of the social ensemble – citizens' inability to conceive, let alone grasp, the totality of social life – combined with the chronic uncertainty of key aspects of life (employment and investment patterns, who will govern after the next elections, the contingent identity of one's self and one's household) makes their members prone to stress, anxiety and revenge. All modern civil societies are more or less caught in the grip of what Heinrich von Kleist called the 'fragile constitution of the world' (*die gebrechliche Einrichtung der Welt*), and such fragility increases the probability that the customary moral sanctions and restraints upon the resort to violence can be rejected or avoided by some of their members. Especially when combined with social discrimination, say in the form of racial prejudice and joblessness, this amoral anxiety and frustration encourages violent responses, sometimes directed by the disadvantaged against themselves. This probably is one reason why the homicide rate for black Americans is seven times higher than for whites, why nearly two-thirds of persons arrested for murder and violent robbery are black and why half the population of US gaols is black, even though blacks represent only 12 per cent of the overall population. The effect of such patterns is to create archipelagos of incivility within an otherwise civil society that contains certain medieval features. Just as in the Middle Ages many men always carried arms, never lightly ventured beyond the towns and feared that the forests were full of frightening foes, so the white middle-class inhabitants of cities such as New York – where there are some 2000 murders each year, a figure nearly as high as the *total* number of killings in the whole of Northern Ireland since the end of the 1960s – never get off the subway in Harlem by mistake, never go to the South Bronx, never take the subway alone after midnight (or earlier, if they are women) and never set foot in Central Park after dark.

The increasing availability and cheapness of means of violence within existing civil societies no doubt fuels this tendency, although the degree to which it does so remains uncertain, which is why hysterical claims about the need for gun control should be tempered with reflection on both the multiple roots and forms of violence and the ways in which the resort to arms is *symptomatic* of the deeper tendency of civil societies to unnerve and disorientate their members. Among the least obvious ways in which the fragile openness of civil societies contributes to their apparently violent character is the way in which their sophisticated means of public and private communication ensure images of violence are circulated more or less freely to large numbers of people. That is to say, freedom of communication within civil society ensures that violence against others can and is often turned into entertainment, that is, made the object of popular fascination, thrill and pleasure. The anomic violence that is regularly produced within civil societies is not always, and sometimes rarely, experienced as loss or a lapse into nothingness. The hard fact is that violence can be experienced as pleasure, as fulfilment, as a form of excitement that tickles the fancy of not only the violated – expressed in masochistic pleasure – but also the violent and the witnesses of acts of violence. Individuals who are violent, alone with their victims, sometimes treat their actions as entertainment, as in the case (described by Arthur Miller) of the misfit 'stuck with his boredom, stuck inside it, stuck to it, until for two or three minutes he "lives"; he goes on a raid around the corner and feels the thrill of risking his skin or his life as he smashes a bottle filled with gasoline on some other kid's head. It is life . . . standing around with nothing coming up is as close to dying as you can get.'[58] Group

[58] Arthur Miller, *The Misfits*, London 1961, p. 51.

pleasure in being violent – exemplified by šljivovica-swilling Serbian soldiers singing their way through scores of daily murders – is frequently reported. So too is the pleasure of those witnessing the spectacle of violence.

Contrary to the claims of contemporary campaigners against violence in the media, the packaging and marketing of violence as entertainment is an old phenomenon traceable to the middle of the eighteenth century. Pay-TV sexual murders, Mortal Kombat video games, vomit-provoking splatter films and musicians who cavort with death, safety pins jammed through their bloodied noses, singing of destruction, midnight ramblers and psychokillers, are ancient themes of modern popular culture. The tradition of entertaining violence stretches back through films such as *Night of the Living Dead* and *Psycho* to magazine ghost stories, horrid melodramas, newspaper sensationalism and the Gothic literature and Graveyard poets of the period of Enlightenment. There is admittedly little research on the history of these public representations of violence, but it is clear that in modern times scandals generated by violence are older than the trials of O.J. Simpson and the Yorkshire Ripper. The scaffold, for example, was a dominant emotive symbol in early nineteenth-century England. The totemic image of the 'hanged man' pervaded popular culture, for instance appearing on tarot cards, in dream books and in Punch and Judy shows; the tanned skin of the executed was used to bind books about his or her crime; and death masks of hanged criminals attracted big crowds at Madame Tussaud's. A parallel transformation of violence into entertainment, this time involving the violated female corpse, was evident in Weimar Germany, whose civil society, consumed by fear of inside and outside threats, was riveted by

Jack the Ripper's deeds in Wedekind's Lulu plays, Otto Dix's paintings of disembowelled prostitutes and Alfred Döblin's sexualization of the murder of Rosa Luxemburg.[59]

With the advent of mass circulation and niche-marketed electronic media operating on a global scale, the age span, size and spatial reach of audiences potentially interested in violent entertainment arguably grows exponentially, to the point where the spectators of violence virtually anywhere in the world can be titillated by hair-raising gore so explicit that it seems unsurpassable in terms of technical perfection and verisimilitude. Why so many millions – gasping and shuddering involuntarily, cold sweat on their brows, upstanding hairs on the nape of their necks – are fascinated by the violent things they might otherwise be expected to run screaming from is an enigma that prima facie lends credence to the originally Freudian thesis of the uncanny (*das Unheimlich*), according to which death, for which there is no known cure and which is the inevitable destiny of all individuals, may well be 'kept from sight . . . withheld from others', but that very rendering of death as a stranger boomerangs on the individual, heightening his or her

---

[59] See the account, which is based upon source materials from newspapers, criminal archives and popular ballads, by Gatrell, *The Hanging Tree*. The nineteenth-century development of unbridled newspaper sensationalism of acts of violence – the insistence on the hot currency of the news, claims for the unique ferocity of murders, the reportage of gruesome details – is traced in Thomas Boyle, *Black Swine in the Sewers of Hampstead: Beneath the Surface of Victorian Sensationalism*, New York 1989. The Weimar fetish of violence against women is documented in Maria Tatar, *Lustmord. Sexual Murder in Weimar Germany*, Princeton, N.J. 1995.

sense that death, the ultimate consequence of violence, is 'uncomfortable, uneasy, gloomy, dismal . . . ghastly'.[60] Freud supposed, misleadingly, that the experience of the uncanny, the primitive fear of the dead that inhabits the strange realm between the living and the dead, was a universal human experience. He did not see that the uncanny in fact assumes different historical forms, and that in premodern systems definitions of the uncanny tend to be monopolized and strictly defined by core institutions such as religious authorities, warrior classes and local communities. Understood in this more historically sensitive way, the theory of the uncanny has a striking implication for theories of the modern civilizing process, which need to be reformulated thus: the invention and growth of modern forms of civil society cannot be described as a process synonymous with the growing invisibility and extrusion of violence into the state sphere. Precisely because the power to define the uncanny is no longer monopolized by well-defined authorities – the uncanny becomes homeless – there develops a *dialectic of civility* in which the visible reduction and practical removal of various forms of violence from civil society coincides with the heightened media visibility and sensuous appreciation of simulated or virtual violence by the citizens of that society, who get qualitatively less solace from worn-out platitudes about salvation and the afterlife.

---

[60] Sigmund Freud, 'The Uncanny' (1919), in *The Standard Edition of the Complete Psychological Works*, James Strachey, ed., London 1955, volume XVII, pp. 219–52.

Child Murder

The pleasurable experience of witnessing 'virtual' acts of violence is one thing; the 'actual' violence committed against others within civil society is another, as now needs to be illustrated. The key point here is that within all civil societies there are times and places in which citizens experience personal confusion and social fatigue, even the feeling that life (as the Russians say) is an empty lawless space (*prostranstvo*); they are therefore tempted to avenge their confusion, frustration and sense of injustice by taking it out on others physically. Two examples – microviolence hidden away in the interstices of civil society (child murder) and macroviolence that spreads to the whole of civil society (nationalism) – should suffice.

Consider the strange phenomenon of child murder: the officially recorded number of child murders in countries such as Britain, France and the United States has substantially increased in recent decades. While doubts about statistics certainly apply – the history of modern household violence against children has yet to be written – the available figures reveal certain new patterns of uncivil treatment of children. During the past forty years in the United States, the recorded number of children murdered during the first year of their lives has doubled; there has been a quadrupling of the murder rate among one- to four-year olds; and among African-Americans more than 20 children in every 100,000 are slain.[61] The trends generate huge media coverage and in consequence child murder, like other forms of violence, appears to move closer to those who previously had

[61] Ros Coward, 'The Heaven and Hell of Modern Motherhood', *The Guardian*, 12 June 1995, p. 13.

heard of, but had never seen, such hideousness. It has come to light that some 60 per cent of those charged with murder are the parents of the child, which casts a lurid light on the cherished term 'blood relations'. Especially anguishing for many commentators are the stories of murderous mothers, trapped in the hell and heaven of contemporary motherhood, who suffocate their children with exhaust fumes, or strap them into safety seats before rolling the family car into a lake, or stab their children to death before taking their own lives.

Many shocked commentators have reacted prepolitically to such dastardly acts. They talk (in the traditional language of the doctrine of original sin) of evil acts, all the while illustrating their point with spine-chilling, Hitchcockian details of the protagonists' lives; or (a not unrelated explanation) their commentaries revive Hobbesian assumptions about the state of nature by highlighting the murderous effects of the 'me-first society' (Newt Gingrich) spawned by the cultural politics of the 1960s. Such commentators would do well to pause before they judge so simple-mindedly. They should study the phenomenon with the Spinozist motto at their side: 'Smile not, lament not, nor condemn; but understand' (*non ridere, non lugere, neque detestari, sed intelligere*); and they should strive to situate their judgements within the potentially fruitful framework of interpretation that links violence with the dynamics of civil societies. In many recorded cases of child murder, it is clear that both victims and villains are trapped in those high-tension zones of civil society where the conflict-ridden logics of the household (intimacy, sexual desire, identity formation, personal habits, marriage, money, the hard work of cooking, cleaning and childcare) interact with, reinforce and often contradict virtually the same list of conflict-ridden logics of the labour market (with its additional, special stresses and strains of employment, unemployment and underemployment) and its neighbouring and crisscrossing social relations with the wider civil society. Seen within the context of these *typical* pressures of civil society, the much-vaunted explanation of evil selfishness fails to acknowledge the contributing factors of confusion, fatigue, ambivalent feelings of love and hate from mothers and fathers whose lack of mutuality and social support (the absence of men from parenting, the lack of state childcare provision, the underprovision of proper benefits for women who have lost the support of men) and whose emotionally and intellectually impoverished visions push them into a cul-de-sac in which the only way out is a crazed decision to murder another member of civil society, and perhaps even themselves. Quite literally, the pressures of civil society kill its offspring.

On Nationalism

The tendency of civil society to kill itself, to degenerate into incivility on a macroscale, is strikingly displayed in the recent resurgence of violent nationalism within the European region. Contrary to the most popular explanation, nationalism is not caused by the periodic re-emergence in the human breast of atavistic instincts of *Blut und Boden*.[62] Such emphasis on the primordial roots of nationalism correctly pinpoints its deeply emotive dimensions, but, devoid of any historical understanding,

[62] The following draws on my 'Nations, Nationalism and Citizens in Europe', *International Social Science Journal*, volume 140, June 1994, pp. 169–84.

it cannot account for why nationalism appears when and where it does. Furthermore, contemporary nationalism of the Serbian or French or English or Georgian variety is not primarily understandable in neo-Marxian terms as the political response of either a beleaguered or expansionist bourgeoisie (Austro-Marxism), or of classes exploited by capitalist imperialism (Tom Nairn) or by the reckless, creative destruction of the global capitalist economy (Slavoj Žižek). Class domination, de-industrialization, unemployment and the formation of a new underclass of anxious citizens are indeed contemporary consequences of civil societies structured by commodity production and exchange, but they do not spontaneously provoke the growth of nationalism. For that to happen, there must be at least some elements of a pre-existing shared sense of nationhood that is in turn capable of manipulation and public deployment by power groups taking advantage of the openness and *déracinement* cultivated by existing social mechanisms.

If nationalist tensions are not entirely blameable upon capitalism then neither are they ultimately traceable to the operations of 'real socialism'. The ruling Communist Party bureaucracies of countries such as Romania, Hungary and Poland undoubtedly stimulated nationalist tendencies in their effort to legitimate their grip on power, but the conclusion that nationalism is a toxic product of communism is unwarranted. Nationalism (as the Magyar resistance to the Habsburg empire and many other examples suggest) predated the era of twentieth-century communism and, besides, in central and eastern Europe nationalism has emerged much more forcefully in the phase of post-communism.

Since the 'velvet revolutions' of 1989–91 the nationalist card has been played not only by Communist parties and organizations struggling to retain their power – Milošević in Serbia, Kravchuk in the Ukraine and Iliescu in Romania are examples. It has been used as frequently by the anti-Communist opponents of the *ancien régime* – Gamsakhurdia in Georgia, Tudjman in Croatia and Yeltsin in Russia – who in this respect share something of fundamental importance with their Communist foes. Both groups have learnt that in the early stages of democratization, when anti-Communists lack money and Communists lack ideas and conviction, nationalism can warm hearts, change minds and win votes, encouraging citizens to embrace a shock-absorbing identity that washes away their sense of futility, encourages 'solidarity of the culpable' (Šiklová) and gives them the feeling of protection against the ongoing disequilibrium and disorientation produced by the first steps towards civil society and political democracy.

In fully functioning civil societies, it could be said, everything is in perpetual motion. Endowed with liberties to criticize and to transform the distribution of power within state and civil institutions, citizens are catapulted into a state of permanent unease which they can cope with, grumble about, turn their backs on, but never fully escape. Civil societies never reach a point of homeostatic equilibrium. They contain difference, openness and constant competition among a plurality of power groups to produce and control the definition of reality. The world of civil society feels as if it is gripped by capaciousness and uncertainty about who does and should govern. Existing relations of power are treated (and understood) as contingent, as lacking transcendental guarantees of absolute certainty and hierarchical order, as a product of institutionally situated actors exercising power within and over their respective milieux.

It is this self-questioning, self-destabilizing quality of civil society which not only provides opportunities for the advocates of national identity to take their case to a wider public. It also increases the magnetism of violent ideologies such as nationalism. Civil society can severely test citizens' shared sense of the unreality of reality, to the point where they may crave the restoration of certainty about reality and become prey to forms of post-prison psychosis (Havel) and morbid attempts to simplify matters, put a stop to pluralism, take refuge in sealed forms of life and foist unity and order onto everybody and everything.

In the European region, nationalism is at present among the most virile and magnetic of these closed systems of life, or what I prefer to call ideologies.[63] Like other ideologies, nationalism is an upwardly mobile, power hungry and potentially violent language game which makes falsely universal claims. It supposes that it is part of the natural order of things and that national identity – the shared experience of a common language or dialect, affection for an ecosystem, and common customs and historical memories – is a biological fact, all the while hiding its own particularity by masking its own conditions of production and attempting to stifle the plurality of nonnational and subnational language games within the established civil society and state in which it thrives.

Nationalism is a scavenger. It feeds upon the pre-existing sense of nationhood within a given

---

[63] John Keane, 'The Modern Democratic Revolution: Reflections on Lyotard's *The Postmodern Condition*', in Andrew Benjamin, ed., *Judging Lyotard*, London and New York 1992, pp. 81–98.

territory, transforming that shared national identity into a bizarre parody of its former self. Nationalism is a pathological form of national identity which tends (as Milorad Pavić points out in *Dictionary of the Khazars*) to destroy its heterogeneity by squeezing the nation into the Nation. Nationalism has a fanatical core. In contrast to national identity, whose boundaries are not fixed and whose tolerance of difference and openness to other forms of life is qualitatively greater, nationalism requires its adherents to believe in themselves and to believe in the belief itself, to believe that they are not alone, that they are members of a community of believers known as the Nation, through which they can achieve immortality. It is as if nationalism requires them and their leader-representatives (as Ernest Renan put it in *Qu'est-ce qu'une Nation?*) to participate in 'un plébiscite de tous les jours'. This level of ideological commitment ensures that nationalism is driven by a bovine will to simplify things, by the kind of instruction issued by Bismarck: 'Germans! Think with your blood!'

If the protagonists of civil society are engaged in a continuous struggle against the simplification of the world, then nationalism is a continuous struggle to undo complexity, a will not to know certain matters, a chosen ignorance – not the ignorance of innocence. It thereby has a tendency to crash into the world, crushing or throttling everything that crosses its path, to defend or to claim territory, to think of land as power and its native inhabitants as a 'single fist' (Ayaz Mutalibov). Nationalism has nothing of the humility of national identity. It feels no shame about the past or the present, for it supposes that only foreigners and 'enemies of the nation' are guilty. It revels in macho glory and fills the national memory with stories of noble ancestors, heroism and bravery in defeat. It feels itself invincible, waves the flag and, if necessary, eagerly bloodies its hands on its enemies.

At the heart of nationalism – and among the most peculiar features of its grammar – is its simultaneous treatment of the Other as everything and nothing. Nationalists warn of the menace to their own way of life posed by the growing presence of aliens. The Other is seen as the knife in the throat of the nation. Nationalists are panicky and driven by friend–foe calculations, suffering from a judgement disorder that convinces them that the 'other nation' lives at their own expense. Nationalists are driven by the feeling that all nations are caught up in an animal struggle for survival, and that only the fittest survive. Every other speech of Jörg Haider of the FPÖ in Austria insinuates that 'East Europeans' are endangering the state, the constitution and democracy. Neo-Nazis in the new half of Germany shout 'Ausländer raus!', liken Poles to hungry pigs, attribute shortages of bicycles to the Vietnamese and lack of food to Jews, and accuse Turks of taking over German communities. French supporters of Jean-Marie Le Pen warn of the Arab 'invasion' of France. Croatian nationalists denounce Serbians as Četniks or as Bolshevik butchers who murder their victims and mutilate their bodies; Serbian nationalists reciprocate by denouncing Croats as Ustaše, fascists who are hell-bent on eliminating the Serbian nation. Both curse Muslims as Islamicized Serbs or Croats, or as foreign invaders of a land in which they have in fact lived for five centuries.

Yet nationalism is not only fearful of the Other. It is also arrogant, confidently portraying the Other as inferior rubbish, as a worthless zero. The Other is seen as unworthy of respect or recognition because its smelly breath, strange food, unhygienic habits, loud and off-beat music and incomprehensible babbling language places it outside and beneath us. It follows that the Other has few if any entitlements, not even when it constitutes a majority or minority of the population resident in the vicinity of our nation. Wherever one member of the Nation is, there is the Nation. It is true (as Lenin emphasized) that the nationalism of a big, conquering nation should be distinguished from the nationalism of those small nations which it conquers, and that conquering nationalism always seems uglier and more culpable. It is also true that nationalism can be more or less militant, and that its substantive themes can be highly variable, ranging from attachment to consumption and a treasured form of currency to boundary-altering forms of political separatism. Yet despite such variations nationalists suffer from a single-minded arrogance. This leads them to taunt and spit at the Other, to label the Other as wogs, *Scheiss* and *tapis*, to discriminate against them in institutional settings, to prohibit the public use of minority languages (linguicide) or even, in the extreme case, to press for the violent expulsion of the Other for the purpose of creating a homogeneous territorial nation.

Uncivil Wars

THIS MURDEROUS reductio ad absurdum of nationalism surfaced in twentieth-century Europe on its southern fringes during and after World War I, with the mass extirpation of Armenians from Turkey in 1915 and, after the crushing defeat of the Greek army by the Turks in Anatolia in 1922, the expulsion by Greece of some 400,000 Turks and a reciprocal expulsion by the Turks of perhaps 1.5 million destitute and panic-stricken Greeks from the lands of Asia Minor, where they had lived with others since the time of Homer. The twentieth century ended with the herding and murdering of nations in south-central-eastern Europe, where, in the early stages of the Balkan conflict, Bosnian Muslims – the Jews of the late twentieth century – were shot at, herded at gunpoint from their burning homes, summarily executed in nearby houses or marched in columns to railway sidings, past rotting corpses, to be trucked off to concentration camps where they were raped or castrated and then made to wait, with bulging eyes and lanternous faces, for the arrival of their own death.

The scale and ferocity of violence produced by such twentieth-century conflicts have fascinated, shocked and sickened the whole world. Words cannot easily describe their cruelty, and their attempted theorization seems at first glance to be a self-indulgent act of blandiloquence. Those who do attempt to reflect on such patterns of violence are easily gripped by feelings of shame that they are uninvited witnesses of events littered by corpses sweet with the smell of doom. Perhaps this experience of uncomprehending shame is one key reason why the kind of modern theorizing of bloody 'civil war' famously initiated by Thomas Hobbes's *Behemoth: The History of The Causes of The Civil Wars of England, and of The Counsels and Artifices By Which They Were Carried On From The Year 1640 To The Year 1660* (1668) has been badly neglected of late. There is today a virtual absence of reflection upon uncivil war, which is scandalous considering the sheer volume of armed conflict that has spread to the four corners of the earth. Admittedly, after the end of the Cold War there is a great deal of confusion about how to interpret these violent conflicts. There is growing agreement that the distinction between war and peace is as questionable now as it was during the Cold War period, but for different reasons. That period, marked by bipolar ideological and geopolitical antagonisms, saw neither war nor peace. While genuine peace, in the sense of the relatively predictable absence of war or threats of war, proved impossible, actual outbreaks of war, even in limited domains, were checked by the serious risks of escalation and of mutual nuclear annihilation; or, as Raymond Aron's favourite formulation expressed it, the Cold War made 'peace impossible, war unlikely'.[64]

By contrast, the recent crumbling of the Soviet empire and of global East-West confrontations has made war rather less improbable. Although a third world war now seems less likely, localized wars have become both more likely and actually more prevalent. If, during the Cold War, neither war nor peace held sway, then the formula for the post-Cold War period, as Pierre Hassner has

[64] The formulation first appeared in Raymond Aron's *Le Grand schisme*, Paris 1948, and was reiterated, shortly before Aron's death, in *Les Dernières années du siècle*, Paris 1984.

put it, is 'both war and peace'.[65] Symptomatic of this enigmatic trend are the garbled developments within Europe itself, whose western regions are engaged in a politics of integration of nation-states aimed at putting an end to war, while a few hundred kilometres to the south-east a most bloody uncivil war with hundreds of thousands of casualties has raged. In this new era, marked by both war and peace, such bloodshed is widespread. It has been estimated that in 1964 there were violent resistance movements in less than a dozen countries – Angola, Cambodia, Congo, Cuba, Cyprus, Guatemala, Laos, New Guinea, Republic of South Africa, Vietnam and Yemen – whereas today the number of such conflicts has, according to reliable recent UN estimates, increased some seven times, to represent nine-tenths of all large-scale armed conflicts around the world.

But not only are local uncivil wars on the increase. In some places, their form and content are undergoing transformations that are not grasped by conventional analyses of so-called civil war. In order to clarify this point, some reflection on the conventional understanding of civil war is necessary. According to the standard social science approach, civil war is conflict within a society resulting from an attempt to seize or maintain state power and its symbols of legitimacy by extralegal, violent means.[66] Civil war is a violent form of

[65] Pierre Hassner, 'La Guerre et la paix', in *La Violence et la paix. De la bombe atomique au nettoyage ethnique*, Paris 1995, pp. 23–61.

[66] The various works by J.K. Zawodny on unconventional warfare well illustrate this approach. See his two-volume *Men and International Relations: Contributions of the Social Sciences to the Study of Conflict and Integration*, San Francisco 1966, and his essay, 'Unconventional Warfare', *American Scholar*, volume 31, 1962, pp. 384–94.

horizontal conflict with vertical aims. It is said to be civil because civilians are engaged in it. It is said to be a form of war because violence is applied by all parties to the conflict. Typically, it is explained, civil war is triggered by the absence of effective formal and informal channels for resolving certain social and political grievances. The consequent sense of frustration or futility or fear of reprisals among sections of the population may lead them to embrace the assumption or conviction that violence is necessary, in which case there follows a carefully planned and executed struggle to seize the means of state power by using rational-calculating violent methods. It is explained that there are usually three phases in any civil war. Phase one sees the building of the structures of a resistance movement, especially order-giving, message-receiving networks. During phase two, the protagonists of civil war use direct violence against their enemies: their sabotage, underground and guerrilla units apply terror at intervals, selectively hitting the brain and nervous system of the enemy power structure – the ruling elites, the communication and transportation centres, the most strategically sensitive industries. The final phase of civil war, when the outcome of the conflict is decided, is that of insurrection, in which the conflict explodes into the open, with coordinated uprisings in various parts of the country. There are probes by the resistance movement to obtain control of either the capital or strategic parts of the country in order to establish some sort of legitimate countergovernment which would act openly on behalf of the organization. This stage is critical, since it compels the resistance to emerge on the streets and fight until it wins or is destroyed. At this point, the insurgents act in large units, and street fighting is conducted according to the rules of infantry tactics. The insurgents' objective is a series of uprisings, spreading like brushfire, intended to destroy the enemy's formal power structure and machinery of violence throughout the whole territory. At some point, the conflict comes to an end, and the civil war normally may be said to have ceased when either one faction forcibly subjugates its opponent (as in the American Civil War), or the warring parties either establish their independence from each other (as in the civil war that led to the separation of Belgium and Holland) or, mutually exhausted and weakened, the protagonists arrange an at least temporary truce (as in the Wars of Roses).

The orthodox literature on civil war is admittedly summarized here in the briefest terms, in order to highlight its inability to grasp the ways in which civil war can easily become, and today is often, a euphemism for the most terrible experience of death and destruction. As far as I can see, no orthodox theorist has dared question the assumption that civil war by definition must take place at the level of the nation-state, or, to put it differently, whether the concept of civil war can for instance be extended downwards to the subnational or microlevel. What is also striking is that so few theorists have enquired whether – to extend an insight of Hobbes – or to what extent the combatants' violent struggle during a so-called civil war can degenerate into a conflagration in which, in violation of the old moral precepts of 'just war' and rational-calculating strategy, the means of violence appear to take on a life of their own and violence consequently becomes an end in itself.

Some of these possibilities have been fruitfully explored in the recent writings of Hans Magnus Enzensberger, Robert Kaplan, Martin van Creveld and others,[67] according to whom the end of the Cold War hastens the decay of conventional armies and the classificatory grid of nation-states; speeds up the emergence of what Kaplan calls 'a jagged-glass pattern of city-states, shanty-states, nebulous and anarchic regionalisms', and reveals the extent to which the heartlands of Europe and other metropolitan regions are in the grip of 'low-intensity conflict' (van Creveld) or what Enzensberger calls 'molecular civil war' (*molekularer Bürgerkrieg*). Local violence in Sölingen, Tower Hamlets, Los Angeles and Marseille disturbingly parallels the large-scale uncivil wars of the former Soviet Union, Africa, Asia and Latin America. Every carriage on a city's underground, says Enzensberger, can become a miniature Bosnia. So too, we could add, do a growing number of geographic places, epitomized by the shanty towns of Rio de Janeiro's Death Triangle, where drug barons and their gunmen impose curfews, decide when people come and go, who lives and who dies, and generally determine who gets what, when and how; and by violent public places like Route 666, a stretch of highway winding from Monticello, Utah, to Gallup, New Mexico, bedevilled by hit-and-run killings, body dumpings and a crazed killer named the Mad Trucker, who local police suspect runs people over for sport. These conflicts are not understandable through conventional categories like class struggle, youth revolt or national liberation. It would also be a scandalous euphemism to call them *civil* wars. While organized

[67] Hans Magnus Enzensberger, *Aussichten auf den Bürgerkrieg*, Suhrkamp Verlag 1993; Martin van Creveld, *The Transformation of War*, New York and Toronto 1991, especially pp. 1–32, 192–227; Robert D. Kaplan, 'The Coming Anarchy', *Atlantic Monthly*, volume 273, number 2, February 1994, pp. 44–76.

bloody wars of the conventional type no doubt persist, at least some of today's battle zones are best described as *a new type of uncivil war* and, as such, prove just how delicate are the threads of civility within the civil societies of the old democracies, the countries newly emerging from dictatorship and regimes hostile to all openness.

These worldwide uncivil wars display disturbingly new common characteristics. Most striking is the way in which the protagonists of violence outwit top-heavy, clumsy and expensively equipped conventional armies by wielding their own reasonably sophisticated means of violence according to no rules except those of destructiveness – of people, property, the infrastructure, places of historical importance, even nature itself. Previous civil wars certainly were bloody, but the bloodshed nearly always had an organized form, as Trotsky, the architect of victory in a civil war in which nine million people died, recognized when likening Soviet power to organized civil war against the landlords, bourgeoisie and kulaks. Some of today's conflicts appear to lack any logic or structure except that of murder on an unlimited scale. It is therefore tempting to describe the metadestructiveness of these battle zones as a late modern regression into 'tribal' or 'primitive' warfare. Kaplan speaks of the emergence of '*re-primitivized man*: warrior societies operating at a time of unprecedented resource scarcity and planetary overcrowding'. The emerging patterns of violence, predicts van Creveld, 'will have more in common with the struggles of primitive tribes than with large-scale conventional war'.

The temptation to think of contemporary uncivil wars as 'primitive' is itself primitive. It should be resisted, because there is much anthropological evidence that wars among hunting and gathering societies had an entirely different logic. In stateless, egalitarian Muslim desert tribes, for example, order among the various horizontally arranged and vertically nested segmentary groups is maintained without political centralization by the cohesion-producing effects of permanent feuding at all levels, a pattern expressed in the maxim, 'I against my brothers, my brothers and I against our cousins, my brothers, cousins and I against the world.'[68] In his parallel reflections upon American Indian societies, Pierre Clastres interpreted the chronic violence among these societies as a reflex means of guaranteeing their members' autonomy and preventing the emergence of oppressive state institutions. 'Primitive society is society against the State insofar as it is society mobilized for war,' he observed, adding the surprising observation that tribal chieftains, who do not exercise power as we moderns know it, are themselves prevented from exploiting war as a means of empowerment because they are engaged in a journey bound ultimately to end in death. 'Each feat of arms hailed and celebrated by the tribe in fact obligates him to aim higher', until the point is reached where, 'realizing the supreme exploit, he thereby obtains, with absolute glory, death.' The practice of sending a lone warrior abroad to attack the enemy camp and to die like a sacred king, 'alone against all', mirrors in inverted form this same principle of 'all against one'; so too does the strange practice of temporarily integrating prisoners of war into society, giving them wives, treating them royally, until the day they are ritually sacrificed and eaten by their captors.[69]

---

[68] Ernest Gellner, *Muslim Society,* Cambridge 1981, pp. 36–69.

[69] Pierre Clastres, *Recherches d'anthropologie politique*, Paris 1980, pp. 206, 232, 237, 234.

Parallel but obviously different rules for apportioning violence in war have been a persistent feature of modern political thought and practice well into the twentieth century. A wise prince, Machiavelli insisted, knows that although 'he will often be necessitated' to act 'contrary to truth, contrary to charity, contrary to humanity, contrary to religion', the maintenance of his government, even in war, requires him to observe 'what is right when he can'.[70] 'Before undertaking war,' wrote Johannes Althusius, 'a magistrate should first check his own judgement and reasoning, and offer prayers to God to arouse and direct the spirit and mind of his subjects and himself to the well-being, utility, and necessity of the church and community, and to avoid all rashness and injustice.'[71] Even Clausewitz offered a secular version of the same argument by emphasizing the primacy of 'moral forces' and 'the intelligence of the personified state' over the violence of war. In at least some of today's uncivil wars, large and small, all these sober restrictions covering the ground rules of war are swept aside. Alibis abound, to be sure, but on the ground and in the air the law of battle is straightforward: kill, rape, pillage, burn, destroy everything that moves, breathes or twitches. Emblematic of this violence without structure and limits – pure violence operating as both means and end – are grisly inner-city disputes – youths stabbed to death in a row over drugs, a couple murdered and then

---

[70] Machiavelli, *The Prince*, p. 66.

[71] Johannes Althusius, *Politica Methodice digesta atque exemplis sacris et profanis illustrata*, Herborn 1603, edited, translated and with an introduction by Frederick S. Carney as *Politics Methodically Set Forth and Illustrated with Sacred and Profane Examples*, Indianapolis 1995, chapter 35, section 10, p. 188.

dismembered, unidentified victims dowsed in petrol and set on fire – or the summary murder and countermurder of innocents in large-scale uncivil wars. The systematic pursuit and massacre of people like animals by killers in Rwanda who had emptied themselves of all thought and morals typifies the same trend. A survivor recalled:

> Then at about 10.00 a.m. the killing began, with machetes and *masus*. . . . The whole place was completely surrounded, the church, the hospital, the trading centre. No-one could escapc. If people fled in a group, they threw a grenade at them. Then they searched the dead bodies for money. I survived a grenade attack. I fell though I was not wounded. I hid in a corner. My husband had already been killed. . . . At about 2.00 p.m. the attackers left to attack the trading centre. The dead bodies were just too many. The place was red. Blood was flowing like water. I could see babies suckling the breasts of their dead mothers.[72]

Such unrestrained killing implies that at least some of the protagonists of the new forms of violence suffer what Hannah Arendt called a radical loss of self. They certainly lack idealism. Like graffiti on the New York subways, their acts of violence are random and mindless. The killers' faces are blank, their words are cynical. Some of them are rendered decorticate by drugs. 'I don't fucking think about it', they say. 'All I know is that Arabs are shit', or 'Niggers are chickenfuckers', they add. Such remarks, familiar to journalists, who commonly have guns waved in their faces, reveal the striking

[72] Testimony by Clementina Murorunkwere, 13 June 1994, reprinted in the African Rights report, *Rwanda: Death, Despair and Defiance*, London 1994, p. 258.

degree to which today's guerrillas are autistic. Unlike the murderous followers of Mussolini, Stalin or Hitler, today's fighters – skinheads who mindlessly firebomb refugee hostels, for example – act as if they are characters in a Céline novel. They are often no-hopers who believe in nothing but their own private fantasies. Their senses are attuned only to violence and, not surprisingly, they are forced to take leave of sense itself. Unafraid of being shot or injured, they are (like the 'Tiger' paramilitaries led by the ex-bank robber Željko 'Arkan' Ražnjatović) self-destructive gangsters driven by 'anger at anything undamaged' (Enzensberger). In consequence, today's uncivil wars tend to produce chaos in their wake. They vandalize the threefold division of government, army and civilians once enforced by conventional warfare and the Westphalian and Philadelphian models. Today's uncivil wars ransack the legal monopoly of armed force long claimed by states; they put an end to the distinction between war and crime, ensuring that conflict degenerates into 'criminal anarchy' (Kaplan), into deathly destruction and self-destruction, typified by the conspicuous poisoning and torching of food by Renamo fighters in a country racked by famine, or by the Četniks who systematically destroy graveyards, rape or sterilize Bosnian women, and boast in front of reporters that they feel nothing but pride that they massacred every patient in one hospital and smashed up its equipment too.

Thinking Remedies

Uncivil wars are the quintessence of incivility, and the extreme, sometimes mind-boggling cruelty they produce highlights a central strategic problem raised by any reflection on contemporary violence: What, if anything, can be done about such gross incivility? Can we envisage a world where there is more civility than at present? Can uncivil war or even violence itself ever be eliminated from human affairs? While it is not the job of political reflection to legislate detailed policy proposals or to advance political strategies and tactics, it can usefully clarify and highlight the probable advantages and disadvantages of responding to these vital questions in certain ways. In the dirty business of violence, political reflection should especially concentrate on defining what should *not* be done and sketching the corresponding ways of thinking and acting that ensure that such mistakes are avoided. So, for example, the prepolitical temptation to resort to pessimistic ontologies ('Individuals are naturally evil', 'We are all creatures of original sin', and so on) or to utopian wishes ('Peace can come, for all men and women are basically good') should be resisted. Although the latter keep alive the important principle of reducing the quantity and intensity of violence in a world riddled with violence, they are as impractical as the imaginings of a John Lennon song cut into the tearful ending of a feature film about the killing fields of Cambodia.

The same charge of impracticality can be levelled at the old tactic in the history of political philosophy of imagining a political community that puts an end once and for all to civil and military violence. Most of these imaginings have been rendered obsolete by the peculiarly modern pressures of state building, civil society formation, weapons technology and international relations among state and nonstate actors. Perhaps the most influential example of such musings is the vision, stretching from Plato's *Republic* to Rousseau's *Considérations sur le gouvernement de Pologne*, of a small political community of patriotic and potentially armed citizens, who live in isolation from other political communities, have no external military or commercial ambitions, and whose concern for nonviolent perfection is matched by a certain superiority complex and mistrust of foreigners, which binds them together into a freedom-loving citizenry of potential warriors emancipated from the curse of war. Rousseau's advice to Count Wielhorski and his fellow Polish representatives on the eve of the first of the three partitions which led, in the period between 1772 and 1795, to the disappearance of that country from the map of Europe, exemplifies this trend: 'Establish the Republic so firmly in the hearts of the Poles that they will maintain her existence despite all the efforts of her oppressors . . . avoid the frippery, the garishness and the luxurious decorations usually found in the courts of kings. . . . Begin by contracting your boundaries . . . devote yourselves to extending and perfecting the system of federal government: the only one which combines the advantages of large and small states,' Rousseau urged, insisting, as he looked back over his shoulder, that 'our distinction between the legal and the military castes was unknown to the ancients. Citizens were neither lawyers nor soldiers nor priests by profession; they performed all these functions as a matter of duty.' The political moral was clear, or so Rousseau thought:

> preserve and revive among your people simple customs and wholesome tastes, and a warlike spirit devoid of ambition. . . . Do not waste your energies in vain negotiations; do not bankrupt yourselves on ambassadors and ministers

> to foreign courts; and do not account alliances and treaties as things of any moment. If you want to keep yourselves free and happy, heads, hearts and arms are what you want; it is they that constitute the power of a state and the prosperity of a people . . . pay little attention to foreign countries, give little heed to commerce; but multiply as far as possible your domestic production and consumption of foodstuffs. . . . Each citizen [including the peasantry] should be a soldier by duty, none by profession. Such was the military system of the Romans; such is that of the Swiss today; such ought to be that of every free state, and particularly of Poland.[73]

The continuous growth of supranational political and economic forces and the spread of unarmed civil societies with divided identities has transformed this Rousseauian vision of autarkic republican states into an unrealizable utopia. So too has the spread of weaponry and military prowess that threatens all four corners of the earth with annihilation – along with the annihilation of Clausewitz's dictum that victory in modern warfare goes to the army that keeps its nerve longer, wills itself to survive and persuades its adversary to lay down arms. Perhaps there is too much exaggeration in Christa Wolf's talk of 'a bomb induced futurelessness', in which even peace of mind for all peoples has become a thing of

---

[73] The quotations are my translations from Jean-Jacques Rousseau, *Considérations sur le gouvernement de Pologne, et sur sa reformation projetée*, London 1782. Rousseau had evidently planned a work on a scheme for a partial federation among the smaller states of Europe, and had at one time intended to include it in the *Contrat social*. He handed a fragment to a French friend, d'Antraigues, who destroyed it in a panic; see C.E. Vaughan, ed., *Political Writings of J.J. Rousseau*, Oxford 1962, p. 135.

the past. But there can be no doubt that it correctly draws attention to the *global* obsolescence of peace through autarky, symbolized by four key military developments unique to the twentieth century: American B-29s in 1945 unloading comprehensive destruction from the unprecedented height of 20,000 feet; the counterdetonation by the Russians of their first atomic bomb in 1949; the Americans' deployment in 1956 of B-52 intercontinental bombers capable of flying round trips to Moscow; and the development, by the early 1960s, of intercontinental ballistic missiles capable of reaching their far-flung targets within half an hour.

The resort to pessimistic ontologies should also be resisted, for they are of absolutely no help in resolving or reducing the problem of incivility and uncivil war. They are in fact best described as a species of the doctrine of original sin stripped of the fear of God. In practice, pessimistic ontologies usually serve as apologias of continuing violence, as in the ideology of Balkanism, which asserts that killing on the scale witnessed in Bosnia-Herzegovina in the 1990s is what one would expect from this region, where after all human nature in all its brutishness has always clutched at the throats of the living, uncensored by the codes of civility enjoyed by more 'civilized' peoples elsewhere. Dogmatic pessimists conclude that human nature *must* be evil for it to fire 120mm mortar shells into crowded marketplaces, producing an almighty explosion followed by a gentle sound like rain or mountain streams, then a split-second's silence as shoppers are blasted off their feet with a force they have never before experienced, limbs and flecks of flesh splattered everywhere, the air thick with the screams of the wounded and dying and the wails of relatives, friends and witnesses.

Such acts of violence are indeed grist to the mill of pessimistic ontologies, which, however, suffer from their indiscriminate acceptance of 'the facts' to prove their fancy, a lack of interest in the motivations of those who kill and are killed and ignorance of the historical foundations of their presumption. At their best, pessimistic ontologies are no better than holding operations, or alibis, and that is why they meld easily into private antidotes to incivility. Their function, whether intended or not, is often to disarm consciences, to persuade others that really nothing can be done, except for the strategy of putting trust in law and order or opting for a private solution (purchasing a corrugated iron garage in Moscow, employing security staff in London or Tokyo or Abidjan, paying protection money to a warlord in Rio de Janeiro), hoping for the best, which in practice means offloading violence onto others.

There are signs, in some regions and many local communities, that pessimistic ontologies are in fact the ideological accomplices of a long-term trend towards the scattering of violence, whereby the day-to-day defence of society against imaginary or actual threats of violence is passing into the hands of a booming security business, to the point where it is even possible to imagine times and places where quite a few states' monopoly of the means of violence will be permanently eroded by, or fundamentally supplemented with, new forms of condottieri. Admittedly this thought should be handled with care, since the long and bloody struggle of modern state builders to monopolize the means of violence within a given territory has constantly been resisted by urban militias, private armies, armed mercantile companies, privateers, fiscal agents and armies of regional lords and rival claimants to royal power.[74] There are nevertheless plenty of documented cases in which the contemporary structures of state power, government policy making and civil society are becoming twisted and deformed into grotesque shapes by gun-wielding gangs and cartels. An extreme instance of this trend are the power structures operated in Colombia by the Cali cartel, which reportedly controls 80 per cent of the world's cocaine production and is lorded over by such figures as El Alacran (Henry Loaiza Ceballos, the Scorpion). No part of Colombia is untouched by these structures. Drugs and guns flow through the veins of its social life, twisting the construction industry, football clubs, the taxi trade, hotels and some newspapers around their violent fingers, which extend as well into the military, the police and the judiciary. During the past five years, more than 1500 politicians and trade union leaders, 1000 police officers, 70 journalists, 4 presidential candidates – out of a field of 6 in 1990 – an attorney general and a governor have been killed by the armed forces and their drug-running paramilitary allies commanded by such figures as El Alacran. The Scorpion himself symbolizes the problem of incivility. Beginning his career as a *sicario*, a hitman, with a reputation for casual ruthlessness, he travelled up through the drug ranks to lead the military wing of the Cali cartel, being implicated in some of its darkest exploits, such as the 1991 massacre of 107 peasants whose bodies were dismembered by chainsaws.[75] Uncorrupted figures who set

[74] Janice E. Thomson, *Mercenaries, Pirates, and Sovereigns. State-Building and Extraterritorial Violence in Early Modern Europe*, Princeton, N.J. 1994.

[75] These events are documented in the Amnesty International

their faces publicly against such thickets of guns, drugs and killings are usually provided with rough treatment – or murdered. In 1983, after being accused in the congress of accepting drug money, Rodrigo Lara Bonilla, the then minister of justice, responded with vehement denials and redoubled attacks on the cartels. Hundreds of drug-transport planes were seized. Arrests were made. Whenever the minister travelled, he would pack and repack his own bags, convinced that someone from a cartel somewhere would plant cocaine on him. His efforts came to nothing. The following year, he was gunned down on the streets of Bogota.

This is of course an extreme example of the contemporary unpicking of the Westphalian model of violent state power. Within both civil and uncivil societies, the possible forms of *condottieri* are highly variable, ranging from uniformed private enterprise security agents wielding walkie-talkies and (where permitted) with guns on their hips, to armed gangs, such as those under the tutelage of rough trade warlords. In every case, however, these private solutions to the dangers of incivility are self-contradictory, since they bring violence, or threatened violence, into the heart of social life. As antidotes to violence, private solutions are also unjust: they serve to offload threatened or actual violence onto others, who are supposed to cope as best they can, if they can. Private solutions always remain private. They relegate some to the probability of cruel encounters and bloody deaths; the lucky others are free to live in luxury in laagers, behind compound walls, surrounded by armed security guards, Balaclavaed soldiers, sniffer dogs, electronic

report, *Political Violence in Colombia: Myth and Reality*, London 1994.

alarms and barbed wire, with loaded guns under the bed.

So the fundamental question remains: Can anything be done to prevent or to reduce uncivil war, particularly when it threatens whole populations? Hans Magnus Enzensberger, Germany's most outspoken and imaginative political essayist, has responded provocatively to this question with a disturbingly modest answer: local fire-fighting is the most that can be done and ought to be attempted. *Hic rhodus, hic salta!* First things first. 'No one would dispute that universal solidarity is a noble goal. Those who are determined to achieve it are to be admired', writes Enzensberger, who strongly criticizes the conviction that citizens and governments of the (formerly colonial) metropolitan countries have heaped so much violence on the rest of the world that they have a duty to remedy violence in far-off countries like Cambodia, South Africa and Colombia. In his view, the guilt-ridden belief that European omnipotence has brought nothing but evil to the world is as suspect as the flip-side conviction that omnipotent Europeans must now deliver good to the world; or as monstrous as the UN Bosnia strategy of refusing to fight the main aggressor, preventing the victims from resisting, all the while trying to protect them against total annihilation. Enzensberger's advice is blunt: abandon the pretentious and guilt-ridden nonsense of universal ethics ('the rhetoric of Universalism') and work for the practical removal of violence in places culturally and geographically close to home. The Germans, for instance, 'cannot solve the situation in Kashmir; we understand little of the conflict between the Sunnis and the Shiites, between the Tamils and the Sinhalese; whatever is to become of Angola must, in the first instance, be decided by the Angolans. And before we get trapped among warring

Bosnians, we ought to mop up the civil war in our own country. Our priority is not Somalia, but Hoyerswerda and Rostock, Mölln and Sölingen.'[76]

Enzensberger is right to insist that building more civility into our civil societies is an urgent and tangible goal. Yet his clear-headed iconoclasm is arguably marred by some wild conclusions that prompt a string of questions central to any plausible reflection on twentieth-century violence: Has traditional civil war actually disappeared from the face of the earth? Is there remaining but a single continuum of senseless violence linking Rostock to Soweto? Are the Kurds who resist Saddam or the Bosnian government troops fighting Serbian gunmen acting like autistic German skinheads or English yobs on the rampage? If not – as seems probable – then surely violent struggles against terror and genocide and sustained efforts to rebuild civility in former war zones make sense? And since some of these struggles – in South Africa, Bosnia and Burma, for instance – have wider and sometimes direct implications for the metropolitan countries and for global power politics, can their citizens and governments simply turn their backs or shrug their shoulders, muttering something about first things first? Or has the problem of cruelty in fact ceased to be a global affair?

Enzensberger seems to respond affirmatively, using the argument that the general containment and reduction of uncivil war is technically impossible, especially in the aftermath of the Cold War. There is just too much violence with which to deal comprehensively. He rejects the whole ideal of 'a policy of world order', like that defended by Stanley Hoffmann, which would require

[76] Enzensberger, *Aussichten auf den Bürgerkrieg*, p. 90.

'that the many sources of global or regional turbulences be dealt with in ways that would minimize violent conflict among states, reduce injustice among and within states, and prevent dangerous violations of rights within them.'[77] Enzensberger is well aware that his own argument is potentially trapped within a performative ethical contradiction (how is it possible to advocate the reduction and tolerance of violence at the same time?), but insists that Gödel's maxim that not even mathematics can save itself from the quagmire of inconsistency applies also to the problem of uncivil war. The selection of priorities is necessary and inevitable. Where to begin? Where can I engage my efforts most effectively? Which of these options should take precedence? Such questions must be at the heart of politico-military initiatives against incivility. Fantasies of omnipotence among politicians, diplomats, generals and citizens should be abandoned by the logic of triage: just as field medicine first categorized the wounded into the three categories of slightly wounded, terminally injured and critically ill in need of priority treatment, so today's uncivil wars are not all remediable. Some require light bandaging by outsiders; others that are incurable have to be left to their own deathly fate; the remainder, those with reasonable prospects of resolution, should preoccupy us.

It is likely that Enzensberger's case, written as it is in spare, angular prose that nurtures ironic understatement, stands within the modern tradition of Jonathan Swift's *A Modest Proposal for Preventing the Children of poor People in Ireland from being a Burden to their Parents or Country; and*

[77] Stanley Hoffman, 'Delusions of World Order', *New York Review of Books*, 9 April 1992, p. 37.

for making them beneficial to the Publick (1729), a tract that has for over two centuries continuously fascinated and shocked its readers with the tongue-in-cheek suggestion that the cruel pauperization of the Irish within the confines of the British empire could be alleviated by the farming of Irish babies for the metropolitan meat market. In certain quarters, Enzensberger's proposed strategy of triage evokes similar shocked outrage, thus confirming his reputation as an exquisite provocateur who knows how to hit his readers where it hurts. That hostile reaction may have been intended by Enzensberger, for (as the controversy whipped up in Germany by his earlier claim in *Der Spiegel* that Saddam was really another Hitler shows) one of his recent preoccupations has been to question the dogmatic prejudice of both naive pacifism and crude-minded militarism. As a political writer who assigns a special role to irony in an age inclined to over-seriousness, Enzensberger, who writes skilfully in many voices, is certainly not a protagonist of parochial apathy. Nor can he be accused of condoning war, by neglect, by advocacy or by untoward comparisons. 'It glistens like the broken beer bottle in the sun/at the bus-stop outside the old people's home', he writes elliptically in a recent poem. War 'rustles like the manuscript of the ghostwriter at the peace conference./ It flickers like the blue reflection of the TV-set/ on somnambulist faces.'[78]

[78] Hans Magnus Enzensberger, 'Der Krieg, wie', in *Kiosk. Neue Gedichte*, Frankfurt am Main 1995, p. 8.

Destruction and Violence

The spirit of Enzensberger's reflections on violence continues where Brecht left off, not with his ideological certainties but with similar acts of lyric *Verfremdung*, in which the observable is poked and prodded and labelled with disturbing understatements, always with an eye for the need for making judgements about the matter at hand. That emphasis on judgement indicates why Enzensberger does not assume that his is the last word on the subject of violence, and why our further reflection on the same theme is not only warranted, but also required. There is certainly plenty of room for theoretically and politically contesting his claims, especially by widening the scope of his concerns (as this reflection on violence has intended) and by extending, sometimes to their limits, his rather vague proposals for coming to terms with the problem of violence as this century draws to an end. Three points – to do with the destructiveness of uncivil war, the importance of cultivating public controversies about violence and the importance of feeling ashamed at what this long century of violence has done to the world – seem especially pertinent.

First, it is important to be clear about the *destructive limits* of uncivil war: to make an effort to highlight the ways in which those who perpetrate violence in bloody, self-destructive form produce disturbing, even absurd outcomes that call into question the legitimacy and efficacy of violence as both the means and ends of power struggles on this scale. It is evident, after a century of increasingly decadent violence, that uncivil wars not only take away life in the present, but that they have life-threatening effects for both those who outlive the conflict and those who are yet to be born. Uncivil wars rule from the grave. Uncivil wars threaten the pact, emphasized by Edmund Burke, between the dead, the living and the unborn, and they therefore destroy the conditions of possibility of civil society in any form. This is true in several ways.

War has often been described as good for business, and there is no doubt that war profiteering remains a chronic feature of armed conflicts around the world – the octopuslike arms trade being the apogee of the whole business. Yet there is a long tradition of modern argument, stretching back well into the eighteenth century, that insists that war is often bad for business, that violence produces decadent forms of investment and that war tends to destroy the infrastructure of market economies, including the civility that is a basic prerequisite of commodity production and exchange. 'I must confess,' wrote David Hume, 'when I see princes and states fighting and quarrelling, amidst their debts, funds, and public mortgages, it always brings to my mind a match of cudgel-playing fought in a China shop.'[79] This old thesis that stagnation or pauperization is the offspring of incivility arguably remains pertinent in the face of widespread incivility and all-out uncivil war, which undoubtedly diverts resources into unproductive, mafia-type activities like corruption and criminality, which in turn weaken or wreck the possibility of developing or sustaining a dynamic economy that can enable citizens to live well. The economic decline of war-torn uncivil societies like Sierra Leone, Lebanon and Algeria not only serves as a reminder that markets function well only when they are embedded in a robust civil society.

---

[79] David Hume, 'Of Public Credit', in *Essays, Moral, Political, and Literary*, T.H. Green and T.H. Grose, eds, London 1898, p. 396.

The inverse rule applies with a vengeance. Uncivil war perversely highlights the point that where there is no civil society there cannot be markets, because market economies are directly dependent upon a dense and delicate forest of nonviolent civil institutions, whose patterns of social solidarity, norms of reciprocity and civic engagement are vital for ensuring flows of information about technological developments, general awareness of the credit worthiness of would-be entrepreneurs, the restriction of get-rich-quick forms of opportunism and, through informal interactions in cafes, bars, clubs and on the streets, the encouragement of workers' motivation, reliability and sense of dignity.[80]

Uncivil wars, the most extreme form of incivility, also have long-term destructive effects upon the ecosystem in which battles rage. T.S. Eliot's premonition (in *The Waste Land*) of an ultimate war where 'the dead tree gives no shelter, the cricket no relief, and the dry stone no sound of water' is no longer mere fantasy. Whether in Kabul or Vukovar or Grozny or Sarajevo, uncivil war leaves behind a trail of ravaged buildings, whole fields of oil-stained earth and piles of toxic rubble where no flowers or trees grow, and where tired, ill-looking men and women bury their dead, leaving the young to grub around elsewhere amidst the rat-infested ruins in search of firewood, flour, nettles and potatoes. The ecological damage caused by uncivil war, old or new, seems to be unaffected by the degree to which fighting is conducted by high-tech or low-tech methods. Many so-called low-intensity conflicts are long-running battles that turn entire regions or countries into theatres of war that not

[80] Robert D. Putnam, *Making Democracy Work. Civic Traditions in Modern Italy*, Princeton, N.J. 1993, pp. 152–62.

only destroy civilians but do long-term ecological damage, aided (as in the widespread dumping of toxic wastes in Lebanon) by organized crime desperate to profit from the breakdown of law and order and public inspection of power. Ecological damage is also a chronic feature of high-tech battle, as in the recent Gulf War, in which the American-led coalition bombing of oil wells and oil tankers in Iraq and Kuwait, and Iraq's torching of oil wells and deliberate pouring of oil into the ocean, left the Persian Gulf area covered for weeks in black acrid smoke filled with sulphur and permanently polluted from biochemical weapons spillages, oil leaks and oil-well fires that took many months to extinguish.

Uncivil wars also do long-term damage to what might be described as the ecology of human personality. Since uncivil wars threaten individuals with death, they always breed fear. Every living creature is drawn into a permanent state of emergency. The conflict resembles a free fire zone, a killing ground, in which everything that moves or impedes free movement is shot at. Hobbes, who recognized the fundamental importance of fear as a factor of politics, supposed that during uncivil wars fear-ridden individuals could and would come to their senses and that they would will themselves rationally into a peace contract, as if conquering fear were merely a matter of mind over body. Things are never so simple. The fear upon which uncivil wars feed can have a warning and mobilizing function. As Hegel remarked, it lifts those who fight or are trapped by fighting, reminding them that there are higher things in life than earthly possessions. Fear enables them to survive, even to act as they never thought they could. Fear can even produce a 'craving for the extraordinary', as Ernst Jünger called the bizarre patterns of reckless solidarity among World War I soldiers who were hell-bent on destroying the cathedrals at Rheims and Albert and who thought nothing of attacking even Notre Dame from the air. We have heard much of war 'heroism' of this kind, but, beginning with Hobbes, we have heard much less of the paralysing and sometimes auto-destructive effects of violence-induced fear upon individuals. Edmund Burke's reply to Hobbes remains salient: 'Civil wars strike deepest of all into the manners of the people. They vitiate their politics; they corrupt their morals; they pervert even the natural taste and relish of equity and justice.'[81]

For every epiphany produced by uncivil war there is at least a handful of psychosomatic casualties. Fear generated by war often devours the souls of citizens, eroding or destroying their capacity to make judgements and act in solidarity, with and against other citizens. The violated are not only permanently tired from spending nights and days in basement shelters. They are also afraid of being frightened, gripped with fear of ceasing to be themselves. They know that violence, unlike Achilles' lance, does not heal the wounds that it inflicts. The violated experience nightmares in a void. Words often fail them, or burn their mouths when they try to speak about their plight. The afraid are haunted by the ghosts of violence, which appear and reappear as extreme trauma syndromes, or as 'air-raid worried minds' (Siegfried Sassoon), or as sickening fears of permanent disablement or probable death (as in the so-called Gulf War Syndrome of weight loss, chronic allergies, seizures and cancers that may have been triggered by the cocktails of vaccinations and anti-nerve gas drugs issued to troops subsequently engaged in Operation Desert

[81] Burke, *A Letter to John Farr and John Harris, Esqrs.*, p. 203.

Storm). Then there are the long-term inner fears that periodically trouble the individual at random. There is a large body of literature describing the low self-esteem, self-destructiveness and willingness to project violence onto others of many children who have witnessed violence or who have been beaten during childhood. It is also well known that women who have been raped or men who have been attacked and robbed on the street suffer occasional nightmares or daytime fits of panic or uncontrolled weeping. Under conditions of uncivil war, such symptoms are experienced far more intensely and for longer periods, certainly well after the objective conditions of violence have disappeared. If and when peace comes, individuals carry uncivil war around within them. They have the sour smell of rotting corpses permanently in their nostrils. They experience no joy in 'victory'. Clinical evidence from the war in Bosnia, although still impressionistic, documents these effects, some of which are enigmatic, including many cases of women who have been raped, but who – it sounds unbelievable at first – sometimes find that fact among the most understandable and therefore least troubling of their worries, and who are instead mainly traumatized by their separation from their children, deeply disturbed by witnessing their husbands shot dead outside their homes, or shattered by the experience of queuing several hours for water, carrying buckets of it up flights of stairs to their make-shift apartments in bombed-out hotels, only to fall victim to the snipers' trick of waiting until the woman arrives at her doorway before shooting a bullet straight through each of her buckets, with flawless precision. Like survivors of holocausts, the violated remain vulnerable to 'deformations, dislocations, and imaginative impediments' in the form of psychic numbing, guilt generated by the escape from death's clutches and a fragmentary understanding of the hard-won experience of survival.[82] The brush with violent death immobilizes them; they are forced to struggle, joylessly, against their own confusions and traumas of the past, their half-articulate, disordered experience of the present world and their damaged expectations of the future, if they are blessed with any.

Uncivil strife normally leaves in its trail another deadly legacy: whole populations and vast tracts of land saturated with unused or unexploded weapons that can prove to be far greater killers in times of peace than in times of war. Uncivil wars help dissolve the distinction between war and peace; peace becomes smouldering war, full of everyday reminders of the persistence of violence. Unexploded mines are a symbol of this problem of the obsolescence of peace, or the persistence of violence long after formal agreements to stop it have been made.[83] Land mines, a gift from the twentieth century to posterity, are of course not new. Designed as a response to the tank during World War I, they were used extensively in World War II, especially in Russia and Poland. Yet these land mines were large and heavy objects that were time-consuming to lay, easily detectable and used mainly against specific military targets; mines were designed to maim or kill enemy troops, to slow their movement and to protect military

[82] Robert Jay Lifton, *The Future of Immortality and Other Essays for a Nuclear Age*, New York 1987, p. 24.

[83] The following draws upon the well-documented report by the Arms Project of Human Rights Watch and Physicians for Human Rights, *Landmines. A Deadly Legacy*, New York, Washington, Los Angeles and London 1993.

installations, troops, civilians and territory. During the 1960s, technical advances made them smaller, lighter and cheaper – the popular P4 MK2 weighs less than three ounces and costs only a few American dollars – and that, combined with their delayed-action potential, encouraged the perception that they could be used offensively: as inexpensive and efficient means of controlling the movement of populations, terrorizing them, emptying the countryside, creating refugee flows and literally crippling the opposing forces. What took a World War II battalion all day to put in place now took a matter of minutes. Laos and Cambodia saw the first large-scale attempts to scatter mines at random; by 1979, when the Soviet Union invaded Afghanistan, land mines had become a standard offensive weapon, distributed as 'scatterables' with ease over wide areas by artillery, rocket or plane.

Mines have since become big business. While accurate figures are difficult to obtain, there are now some fifty different models, manufactured by around a hundred companies in at least forty-eight different countries, the principal producers and exporters among which are the United States, Italy, Germany, China, Egypt, Singapore and Pakistan. The consequent ease with which land mines can be procured, especially by cash-starved armies, makes their use a standard feature of uncivil wars, with macabre consequences. In Kurdistan, more than half of the total expenditure on health goes to treating and caring for the victims of mines. In Cambodia, there are reportedly thirty thousand amputees in a population of eight million. As elsewhere, more than half are boys and girls blown up while engaged in the rural tasks they have always performed – taking flocks to graze pastures, collecting water and firewood – or while playing. In the early days of the war in Afghanistan, before they knew better, playful children were even attracted to the small, brightly painted, air-delivered mines, nicknamed 'butterflies' or 'green parrots', that rained down throughout the country, which is now littered with an estimated ten million unexploded mines that have destroyed much of the country's irrigation system and the population's self-sufficiency in food. In Angola, where uncivil war has raged for more than three decades, famine has spread through districts too heavily mined to be cultivated. And in war-ravaged Mozambique, where the already huge number of maimed grows daily, repeated mining and countermining by both the Frelimo government and Renamo forces has paralysed transport systems, permanently severed the country's electricity power supplies, forcibly prevented more than two million refugees from returning to their homes and destroyed the tourist industry by killing large numbers of elephants and other wild life in the contaminated game parks.

It is obvious that land mines kill and maim subjects; and that they also choke off the possible future growth of a civil society enjoying a good measure of civility. Land mines can lie dormant for up to two or three decades before being detonated by a child at play, an elderly civilian strolling at dusk or a household pig fattening itself on local fields. The wounds they inflict are ruinous. The shock wave from an exploding land mine often destroys blood vessels well up the leg, forcing surgeons to amputate much higher than the site of the primary wound. Land mines also cause secondary infections by driving dirt, clothing, bacteria, metal and plastic fragments into the body's tissues. Survivors of mine explosions suffer intense physical pain and, frequently, loss of their livelihoods. Their households are confronted with severe financial stress caused by the substantial costs of treatment and rehabilitation, loss of the victim's earnings and the long-term costs of supporting an unproductive relative. In areas prickling with mines, especially rural areas, citizens must either learn to live with mines, working their fields as best they can, risking death each day, or abandon their homes to live safely elsewhere, thereby depopulating the local area and weakening the basis of social solidarity.

Clearing the mines menace is not an easy alternative. Land mines may come cheap, but their average cost of safe removal is somewhere between $300 and $1000 each – a ratio frightening in its implications for a world in which annual per capita income is often less than that, in which there are roughly 100 million uncleared mines, and in which mines are being laid far faster than they are being removed. The effective banning of their production, export, stockpiling and deployment is nowhere in sight – a depressing indication of which is the UN's Landmines Protocol of 1983, which feebly attempted to regulate their use, but not production or sale. Although its provisions are intended to diminish land-mine use against civilians, the protocol contains no enforcement mechanisms and ignores the fundamental problem of temporal randomness inherent in mine warfare: the effects of mines that outlast their military utility and place civilians at risk, typically on a long-term basis. In the meantime, mine clearance remains a primitive process, with no 'silver bullets' in sight. Paradoxically, sophisticated anti-handling devices, often with electronic sensors or microchips, increase the risk to deminers. 'Most mine-clearing tools are glorified farm implements', observes *The Bulletin of the Atomic Scientists*, and 'a man with a stick is still the most common instrument.'[84] Needless to say, the hand removal of mines is dangerous and time consuming, especially given that the people doing it have little idea of the type or location of the mines. The strong political temptation, especially in regions exhausted by war, is therefore to forget the whole dirty business – and violently suffer its consequences in so-called peacetime.

Publicity and Violence

There are many possible methods of dealing effectively with incivility in both its milder and murderous forms. Legislatorlike theoretical reflection on these methods is again unwise since, as has already been emphasized, they necessarily will vary according to time and place and the particular form of violence in question. For instance, certain uncivil wars may only be stoppable through outside military intervention, whereas others may be best ended, with a minimum of violence and a maximum of justice, by the withdrawal of outside forces. In certain contexts, Bosnia-Herzegovina for instance, the practical construction of something like a sovereign territorial state is a fundamental condition of the cessation of uncivil war and the re-creation of the molecular structures of a civil society; in other contexts, for instance the trumped-up battle of Britain against Argentina in the Malvinas war, attempts to shore up the fiction of a sovereign territorial state have bizarre consequences that end in pointless

[84] Jim Wurst, 'Ten Million Tragedies, One Step at a Time', *The Bulletin of the Atomic Scientists*, July/August 1993, p. 20.

bloodshed. By contrast, in milder cases of incivility, common assaults for example, those who have committed an act of violence can be arrested by the police, questioned, released with a caution or dealt with through the law courts and perhaps imprisoned; and so on.

In the face of such complexity, the political goal of reducing and eliminating violence will be effective only to the extent that it tries to cultivate a plurality of strategies, ranging from macrolevel agreements concerning arms reduction, war crimes tribunals and the need for regional integration of previously sovereign states, to microlevel laws against bodily harassment and everyday violence, for instance against women, ethnic groups, gays and lesbians. In every case, or so I want to argue, these tactics will remain inadequately developed or less than effective – or more likely drift into authoritarian 'law and order' strategies – unless cultures of civility are cultivated at the level of civil society. The danger of authoritarianism should not be underestimated, for especially in the old democracies there are presently signs of a strengthening consensus that criminal violence is a growing pathology, and that its obscure causes place it beyond realistic hope of remedy. 'The very high crime rate of young black males is an aspect of the pathological situation of the black underclass, but there do not appear to be any remedies for this situation that are at once politically feasible and likely to work,' writes a well-known Chief Judge in the US Court of Appeals, adding that 'there is no feasible method of preventing parents from beating their children, and also it is unclear whether the beating causes the later violence or the beating and the violence are consequences of the genetic endowment shared by the parents and their children.' These premises lead easily to the conclusion that violence should greet violence. 'Decades of unsuccessful experimentation with different types of rehabilitative programmes have demonstrated the practical futility of the rehabilitative approach and, in the process, have largely discredited criminology as a discipline.' It is said that multivariate data analyses conducted by social scientists prove that 'punishment reduces crime both through deterrence and through incapacitation', and it follows that getting tougher is the right course of action. Juries should be invited to infer from criminal defendants' refusals to testify that they have something to hide. Evidence obtained by the authorities in violation of the law should be considered reliable. Consideration should be given to extending the death penalty to crimes other than unusually brutal or wanton murders. And the costly protraction of criminal proceedings, especially in death cases, where (in the United States) intervals of ten years between sentence and execution are common and intervals of twenty years are not uncommon, must be stopped.[85]

The premise and conclusion of this type of reasoning are questionable, and certainly if its authoritarian or 'get violent with violence' potential is to be contained the task of fostering widespread recognition of the various kinds of negative effects of incivility and the wide-ranging and more or less effective remedies for incivility is arguably a key priority. I want to emphasize that the cultivation of *public spheres of controversy*, in which the violent exercise of power is monitored nonviolently by citizens, is a basic condition for reducing or eliminating

[85] Richard Posner, 'The Most Punitive Nation. A Few Modest Proposals for Lowering the US Crime Rate', *The Times Literary Supplement*, number 4822, 1 September 1995, pp. 3–4.

incivility and for minimizing the chances of its return, in no small measure because of the quadruple propensity of public spheres: to cultivate shared memories of times past when terrible things were done to people; to heighten citizens' and governments' awareness of the nature and extent of actually existing incivilities; to canvass and circulate to other citizens ethical judgements about whether or not (or under what conditions) a certain form of violence is justified; and to encourage the formulation of remedies for incivility, particularly those that are mindful of the complexity of the whole subject and the troubling implications of violence for democratic institutions.

To link violence and public spheres of controversy is to rediscover a theme of Western political thought that is traceable to the Roman legal system, with its emphasis on the inviolability of peacefully negotiated agreements and treaties (*pacta sunt servanda*), and ultimately to the Greek conviction that public life and violence had nothing in common, essentially because men distinguish themselves from the animals by virtue of their capacity for speech (*lexis*) and action (*praxis*) and, thus, by their propensity for publicly banding together into a *polis* of citizens protected from physical violence by walls around their city. This categorical tension between violence and public speech and action was subsequently revived and made a prominent feature of earlier modern political thought, in which three interrelated meanings of 'the public' are identifiable.[86] The public sphere concept was initially bound up with the

[86] I am here summarizing my 'Structural Transformations of the Public Sphere', *The Communication Review*, volume 1, no. 1, Summer 1995, pp. 1–22.

struggle against despotic states in the European region. The language of 'the public', 'public virtue' and 'public opinion' was directed against monarchs and courts suspected of acting arbitrarily, abusing their power violently and furthering their private, selfish interests at the expense of the realm. During the seventeenth and eighteenth centuries, for example, the normative ideal of the public sphere – a realm of life in which citizens invented their identities under the shadow of state power – was a central theme of republicans like the Commonwealthmen, who simultaneously looked back to the Roman republic (and sometimes to the Greek *polis*) and forward to a world without mean-spirited executive power, standing armies and bloody struggles caused by clericalism. With the growing power and dynamism of modern capitalist economies, the ideal of the public sphere later came to be used, for example in Ferdinand Tönnies's *Kritik der öffentlichen Meinung* (1922), principally to criticize organized capitalism, advertising agencies and other institutions bent on divining 'public opinion' and making it speak in their favour. Common to this phase of usage of the concept of public life is less concern with violence and more insistence that commodity-structured economies encourage moral selfishness and disregard of the public good; maximize the time citizens are compulsorily bound to paid labour, thereby making it difficult for them to be involved as citizens in public life; and promote ignorance and deception through profit-driven media manipulation.

If the first two phases of the modern definition of the public sphere highlighted, respectively, the uniquely modern problems of territorially defined state power unaccountable to its citizens and the business-biased egoism of organized market capitalism, then during the third, most recent phase of usage of the public sphere concept these twin problems are simultaneously emphasized. The public sphere ideal is linked to the institutions of public service broadcasting, whose prototype was the BBC; these broadcasting institutions are seen to have an elective affinity with public life because they represent to the whole political community its own hopes and fears and diverse forms of life and opinion, thereby guaranteeing the survival of public values and public controversies in the era of state-organized, consumer capitalism.

Common to each of these modern interpretations of the public sphere is the questionable belief in the ideal of a single, spatially integrated public sphere operating within a nation-state framework. This ideal of a territorially bounded republic of citizens striving nonviolently to live up to their definition of the public good is arguably obsolete. We are living in times in which spatial frameworks of communication are in a state of upheaval. The old dominance of territorially bounded, state-structured public life mediated by radio, television, newspapers and books is coming to an end. In its place, public life today is subject to a marked process of scattering and deterritorialization, in the sense of the development of a complex mosaic of differently sized, overlapping and interconnected public spheres that force us radically to revise our understanding of public life and its accompanying terms such as public opinion, the public good and the public/private distinction.

Although these public spheres emerge within differently sized milieux in the nooks and crannies of civil societies and states, all of them are interested stages of action that display the essential characteristics of a public sphere. A public sphere allows a particular type of spatial relationship between two or more people, usually connected by a certain means of communication (television, radio, satellite, fax, telephone, and so on), in which non-violent controversies erupt, for a brief or more extended period, concerning the power relations operating within their given milieu of interaction and/or within the wider milieux of social and political structures in which the disputants are situated. Public spheres in this sense never appear in pure form – the following description is ideal-typical – and they rarely appear in isolation. Although they typically have a networked, interconnected character, contemporary public spheres have a fractured quality which is not being overcome by some broader trend towards an integrated public sphere. The examples selected below, mainly from the old democracies, illustrate their heterogeneity and variable size, and that is why I choose, at the risk of being misunderstood, to distinguish among *micropublic spheres* in which there are dozens, hundreds or thousands of disputants interacting at the sub-nation-state level; *mesopublic spheres* which normally comprise millions of people interacting at the level of the nation-state framework; and *macropublic spheres* which normally encompass hundreds of millions and even billions of people enmeshed in disputes at the supranational and global levels of power. I should like to examine each in turn, and to explore their implications for theorizations of violence.

The coffee house, town meeting and literary circle, in which early modern public spheres developed at the microlevel, today find their counterparts in a wide variety of local spaces in which citizens enter into disputes about who does and who ought to get what, when and how. Local community meetings of angry Turkish-speaking Germans in Berlin to discuss what can be done about their verbal and physical harassment in schools, supermarkets and on the streets is one example. Another is early American rap music's clever attacks on police brutality and harassment, evident in K. R. S.-One's 'Who Protects Us From You?', a militant philosophical rap using lyrics like 'Killing blacks and calling it the law' and 'every time you say "that's illegal", does it mean that it's true?' Micropublic spheres are also today a vital feature of all contemporary social movements preoccupied with violence. The women's movement, for instance, comprises mainly low-profile networks of small groups, organizations, initiatives, local contacts and friendships submerged in everyday life. These submerged networks, in which women are mainly involved on a part-time basis, constitute the laboratories in which the dominant masculine codes are challenged and new experiences are invented and popularized. Within these local laboratories, the women's movement has utilized a variety of means of communication (telephones, faxes, photocopiers, camcorders, videos, personal computers) to question and undo the dominant power of men, including their violation of women's bodies. These laboratories comprise such public spheres as the discussion circle, the publishing house, the professional women's association, the clinic, the refuge for battered women and the chat about men over a drink with women friends and acquaintances. On occasion, these public spheres coalesce into publicly visible media events, such as demonstrations in favour of abortion or lesbian rights or sit-ins against judges. But, paradoxically, these micropublic spheres that problematize incivility draw their strength from the fact that they are mostly latent. Although they appear to be private, acting at a distance from official public life, party politics and the glare of media publicity, they in fact display all the characteristics of small group public efforts, whose challenge to the existing distribution of uncivil power can be effective exactly because they operate unhindered in the unnewsworthy nooks and crannies of civil society.

Mesopublic spheres are those spaces of nonviolent controversy about (violent) power that encompass millions of people watching, reading or listening across vast distances. They are mainly coextensive with the nation-state, but they may also extend beyond its boundaries to encompass neighbouring audiences (as in the case of German-language programming and publishing in Austria); their reach may also be limited to regions within states, as in the non-Castilian-speaking regions of Spain like Catalonia and the Basque country. Mesopublic spheres are mediated by large-circulation newspapers such as *The New York Times*, *Le Monde*, *Die Zeit*, the *Globe and Mail* and the Catalan daily, *Avui*. They are also mediated by electronic broadcasters such as BBC radio and television, Swedish Radio, RAI and (in the United States) National Public Radio and the four national networks (CBS, NBC, ABC and Fox).

Although constantly pressured from below by micropublic spheres, mesopublic spheres of controversy about violence – concerning such matters as uncivil war, nuclear weapons and urban violence – display considerable tenacity. There is no necessary zero-sum relationship between these differently sized public domains, in part because each feeds upon tensions with the other (readers of national newspapers, for instance, may and do consult locally produced magazines or bulletins, precisely because of their different themes and emphases); in part because mesopublic spheres thrive upon media which appeal to particular national or regional language groupings, and which have well-established and powerful production and distribution structures that sustain their proven ability to circulate to millions of people certain types of news, current affairs, films and entertainment that daily reinforce certain styles and habits of communication about incivility and other matters of public concern; and also in part because public controversies about violent power are regularly facilitated by the privately controlled media of civil society. There is plenty of evidence that just as public service media are ever more subject to market forces, market-led media are subject to a long-term process of self-politicization, in the sense that they are forced to address matters of concern to citizens capable of distinguishing between market hype and public controversies. The British tabloids' ruthless probing and exploitation of murder, rape and other forms of criminal violence is an instance of this trend. So also are popular American current affairs programmes such as CNN's 'Larry King Live' and the remarkable proliferation of fast-cut television talk shows like 'Ricki Lake', which, amidst advertisements for commodities such as chocolates, mattresses and pizza, simulate raucous domestic quarrels about matters such as child abuse, cruelty to animals and gay violence, in front of selected audiences who argue bitterly amongst themselves and, amidst uproar, talk back to the presenter, shout at experts and question the veracity of the interviewees.

The recent growth of macropublic spheres at the global or regional (for example, European Union) level is among the most striking, least researched developments of great interest to reflections on the relationship between violence and publicity. Macropublics of hundreds of millions of citizens are the unintended consequence of the international concentration of mass media firms previously owned and operated at the nation-state level. The current globalization of media firms entails the chain ownership of newspapers, cross-ownership of newspapers, the acquisition of media by ordinary industrial concerns and, significantly, the regional and global development of satellite-linked communications systems. Among the central ironies of this risk-driven, profit-calculating process is its nurturing of public controversies beyond the boundaries of the nation-state. Most of these public spheres are so far fledglings. They operate briefly and informally; they have few guaranteed sources of funding and legal protection, and are therefore highly fragile, often fleeting phenomena. Internationally staged media events like peace conferences, nuclear tests and uncivil wars are cases in point. They are highly charged symbolic events covered by the entire media of the world and addressed primarily to a fictive world audience. During the three major summits hosted by Reagan and Gorbachev, at Geneva in 1985, Washington in 1987 and Moscow in 1988, for example, audiences straddling the globe watched as media such as CNN, ABC's 'Nightline' and the Soviet morning programme '90 Minutes' relayed versions of events that signalled the end of the Cold War.

It is commonly objected that media coverage of violence spreads rituals of pacification, rendering global audiences mute in their fascination with the spectacle of the event. That could indeed be legitimately said of the heavily censored Malvinas War and Gulf War coverages. But there are signs that the globalcasting of summits and other events often tends to be conducted in the subjunctive tense, in that they heighten audiences' sense that the existing 'laws' of power politics are far from 'natural' and that the shape of the world is therefore dependent in part on current efforts to refashion it violently or nonviolently, according to certain criteria.

The dramatic emphasis upon the subjunctive, combined with the prospect of reaching a worldwide audience, can incite new public controversies about violent power stretching beyond the limited boundaries of mesopublic spheres. Probably the most dramatic example so far is the Tiananmen crisis in China during the late spring of 1989. Broadcast live by CNN, twenty-four hours a day, the Tiananmen episode was a turning point in the development of global news. Not only was it perceived as the most important news story yet to be covered by international satellite television. It was also the first occasion ever when satellite television directly shaped the events themselves, which unfolded rapidly on three planes: within national boundaries, throughout global diplomatic circles and on the stage of international public arguments about how to resolve the crisis. CNN's wire-service-like commitment to bring its viewers all significant stories from all sides of the political spectrum helped to publicize the demands of the students, many of whom had travelled abroad and understood well the political potential of the television medium in establishing public spheres in opposition to the totalitarian Chinese state. Not coincidentally, they chose 'The Goddess of Democracy' as their central symbol, while their placards carried quotations from Abraham Lincoln and others, all in English for the benefit of Western audiences. The students reckoned, accurately, that by keeping the cameras and cellular telephones (and, later, 8mm 'handicams' carried around on bicycles) trained on themselves they would maximize the chances of their survival and international recognition. Their cause may in retrospect prove to have been a significant turning point in the eventual collapse of the authority of the Chinese Communist Party. The students' cause certainly won international recognition at the time from other states and citizens, and it also probably prolonged the life of the protest that ended in the massacre of between four hundred and eight hundred students. According to CNN's Alec Miran, who was executive producer in China during the crisis, 'People were coming up to us in the street, telling us to "Keep going, keep broadcasting, they won't come in while you're on the air". That turned out to be true. The troops went in after our cameras were shut down.'[87]

Like all lines of enquiry that transgress the limits of conventional wisdom, the attempt radically to rethink the theory of the public sphere and to link it to matters of power and violence opens up new bundles of tough objections and hard questions, with important implications for future research in the fields of philosophy, politics and communications. The most obvious implication is that the neorepublican attempt to tie the theory of the public sphere to the institution of public service broadcasting has failed on empirical and normative grounds and that, more positively, there are empirical reasons alone why the concept of public spheres should be brought to bear on phenomena as disparate as citizens' initiatives, newspaper-driven murder scandals, satellite broadcasting and uncivil wars anywhere on the face of the earth. Public spheres are not exclusively housed within state-protected public service

---

[87] Cited in Lewis A. Friedland, *Covering the World: International Television News Services*, New York 1992, p. 5.

media; nor (contrary to Habermas) are they somehow definitionally tied to the zone of social life narrowly wedged between the world of power and money (state/economy) and the prepolitical group associations of civil society. The political geography supposed by conventional theories of the public sphere is inadequate. Public spheres can and do develop within various realms of civil society and state institutions, including within the supposed enemy territory of consumer markets and within the world of power that lies beyond the reach of nation-states, the Hobbesian world conventionally dominated by shadowy agreements, suited diplomacy, business transactions and war and rumours of war.

Whether and to what extent there is a long-term tendency for modern public spheres to spread into areas of life previously immune from controversies about power and violence is necessarily a subject for a larger enquiry. It would certainly seem that there are few or no remaining areas of social or political life automatically protected against public controversies about the violence they contain. The early modern attempt to represent the violence associated with patterns of property ownership, market conditions, household life and events like birth and death as 'natural' is in retreat. So too is the older, originally Greek assumption that the public sphere of citizenship necessarily rests on the tight-lipped privacy (literally the idiocy) of the *oikos*. As the process of mediated publicity spreads – television talk shows like 'Ricki Lake' and feminist confrontations with male violence suggest – supposedly private power and violence are being drawn into the vortices of negotiated controversy that are the hallmarks of public spaces. The realm of privacy disappears; the division between 'the public' (where power controversies are reckoned to be the legitimate business of others) and 'the private' (where such controversy is said to have no legitimate role before the thrones of intimacy or individual choice or God-given or biological naturalness) collapses. Politicization exposes the arbitrariness and hidden violence of traditional definitions of 'the private', making it harder (as various figures of power are today painfully learning) to justify any act of violence as nobody else's business.

Guilt and Shame

This growing publicization of violence throws some doubt on the customary view that the increasing saturation of everyday life with media-driven images, particularly those depicting acts of violence, implicates audiences who know no better in a sadomasochistic relationship with that violence. The title of Jean Baudrillard's *The Evil Demon of Images* anticipates this customary thesis: the old adage that war is the continuation of politics by violent means needs to be amended, Baudrillard argues, because media images are now the continuation of war by other means. War, the most concentrated form of violence, has become cinematographic and televisual, just as the mechanically produced image (a film like Francis Ford Coppola's *Apocalypse Now*, for instance) makes war on the world by first devouring everything and everybody in its path during filming, then spewing it out as a mass spectacle of riveting images of napalm, gassed bodies, burned-out tanks, roaring jets, explosions, screaming children, stories of rape and pillage. 'War becomes film, film becomes war.' It is still widely thought that pictures of war bear witness to the world by literally reproducing it as it really is. That is not so,

Baudrillard insists. The image, whether photographic, cinematic or televisual, in fact seduces its producers and consumers by promoting spontaneous confidence in its own realism. The dirty reality of war is thereby discursively swallowed up into a black hole of images which extinguish all referentiality and implode basic polarities such as subject/object, private/public, good/evil and the imaginary/the real. War becomes unquestionable. Images of violence cease to have a transcendent meaning: they are simply actually existing violence. Audiences are seduced and captured and held hostage by such images; images of violence fill them with 'a kind of primal pleasure, of anthropological joy in images, a kind of brute fascination unencumbered by aesthetic, moral, social or political judgements.'[88] Enzensberger's *Aussichten auf den Bürgerkrieg* replicates the same thesis. Television has become 'a single huge piece of graffiti' which serves up massacre as mass entertainment. Acts of violence in Sarajevo, Kigali, Belfast and elsewhere in effect function as 'a horror movie with its own blood-and-guts productions'. Scenes of broken-hearted refugees, raped and ravaged by raging battles in faraway countries, and footage of desperate violence within the broken-down hearts of sophisticated cities are not treated with the gravity or sophistication they deserve. They become light entertainment.

The extravagant thesis is implausible, for several reasons other than the proliferation of public spheres of controversy about violence sketched above. If the violence-as-mass entertainment theory were literally true, then it is unclear how the apocalyptic theory itself could explain how it has emerged unscathed from

[88] Jean Baudrillard, *The Evil Demon of Images*, Sydney 1988.

a world in which all meaning has become enveloped within the mass media. If the theory were literally true, that is if it was not a deliberately exaggerated provocation, then it is also unclear what should be done about the phenomenon, except, supposing its undesirability, to ban all mass media reportage of violence (a possible recommendation that might well be implied by Enzensberger's call for citizens to forget about the wider world and to concentrate upon the forms of uncivil war closest to home). The thesis also says nothing about the survival and flourishing of the uncanny under pressures from the modern civilizing process; and it rests as well upon an unspoken assumption about the nitwit nature of the viewing audience. It supposes that the audience comprises hapless and gullible idiots who are incapable of interpreting or reinterpreting images of violence, even those which are presented with explanations of their origins, causes and ethical implications, and that the audience is therefore at most capable of catharsis, or gross satisfaction in the misfortune of others. This assumption that audiences are stupid misanthropes flies in the face of considerable counterevidence that they sometimes experience moral revulsion at the violent images with which they are confronted; and that they either take steps to turn away from such images or avoid them as far as possible or draw their own conclusions, often by talking with others, about both the programme format and story itself as well as the pros and cons of the violence in question.

The doubt about the Enzensberger/Baudrillard thesis can be put differently. It supposes that visual representations of incivility and uncivil war are seamless texts that always overwhelm those who sit still before them –

dissolving the audience into a fictional nothingness. It must be admitted that audiences are sometimes seduced and objectified by texts that appear seamless, but the overall supposition that the category 'audience' has been abolished is implausible, not only for empirical reasons (controversies about violence still abound) but also because the supposition conflates the different modes of textual representation of violence and, hence, understates the probability of different modes of audience response to that violence. Some texts about violence are state-centred and subject to heavy censorship; others are more or less journalist-centred or produced from the points of view of the perpetrators or victims of violence; and still others may be an eclectic mixture of some or all of these possibilities. Not only that, but within each of these types of representation of violence there is a codified 'intention of the text' (Eco) which as it were codetermines or divines particular types of responses by the interpreting audiences exposed to the violence. There is never just one definitive meaning of any media account of a violent episode, and certainly not that of the author of the particular account; there are only ever plausible or implausible interpretations of the communicated episode, that is, more or less persuasive judgements that are prestructured by the form and content of the media account itself. Some media narratives, the heavily censored British television coverage of the Malvinas War, for example, encourage flag waving and the glorification of violence by their audiences; others, for instance slick televisual news coverage of a rape or murder in the local community, induce paralysing shock or puzzlement or sickening depression that serves to contain audience responses within strictly defined limits; still other narratives suppose audiences can be shocked by the cruelty of the violent and encourage those audiences to empathize with the violated and/or to engage not merely in 'understanding' the violated but also to 'overstand' the narratives; that is, to engage in a kind of questioning of the facts behind the facts of the violence that the narratives themselves do *not* encourage audiences to ask.

Media narratives that highlight representations of resistance to violence are a case in point of the latter possibility. Televisual images of violence never simply highlight the destructiveness of violence. We see not only burning, looting, killing, rubbled buildings, bloodied bodies, but also images of the first green shoots of civil society within an uncivil war zone: shoes being fashioned from the tyres of a bombed-out car; people tidying up flats whose entire walls have been blown away; a woman looking through rubbish tips for rags to use as nappies; a postman who appears from nowhere; a priest gathering around him ragged-trousered youths to set up a car repair workshop in a ramshackle shed next to his war-damaged church. Less obvious are those diffuse or more subtle forms of resistance evidenced on the screen, including the independently minded reporter/journalist, whose face shows signs of stress and whose voice connotes bravery and empathy with his or her victims. Then there is the victims' silence, the eerie stillness of those whose violation cannot be spoken of, let alone described; and, linked somehow to their silence, their cries, voiceless cries which are evidently addressed to no one and everyone in particular. The cries of the violated, no matter where they are located on the face of the earth, have never been transmitted so frequently or so widely to such large audiences as they are nowadays. Some of them – Nick Ut's 1972 photograph of the screaming naked girl fleeing from her napalmed village in Vietnam is an example – have become iconic. Those cries have uncertain effects, to be sure. Those who cry never know whether they will be heard, let alone understood. But arguably that is why they can be so powerful. Crying exceeds all language, not only in the primeval suddenness with which it breaks the silence surrounding the violence that has been perpetrated, but also in its militant disregard for the grammar of language. Crying never comes to a halt, as if it were reduced to gibberish. It stands outside the boundaries of linguistic sense, echoing in the ears of those who hear, its meanings infinitely suspended and never fully decipherable. Crying cries out indefinitely to be heard, to be understood, to be remedied.

The crying of those who have been violated sometimes – or often – triggers questions about responsibility among those who see or hear the grief of those who cry. Why and to what extent such a conversion process takes place remains something of an enigma to social scientists, and to publics at large. Empathy with the violated happens, but why and when and for how long remains utterly unpredictable. All that is known is that it happens, and that to the extent that it does we can speak of a hidden, potentially civilizing dialectic within the growing trend towards ever-increasing media coverage of virtually all forms of violence. This media-nurtured sense of responsibility for the fate of the violated among those who witness violence can be accompanied by several emotions, of which not only denial ('I am not responsible for these horrors') and helpless confusion ('What can I possibly do?') but also *guilt* and *shame* are significant possibilities. In the English vernacular, these latter words are often confused, but the markedly different dispositions they signify should be distinguished within any contemporary theorization of violence.[89] Guilt, the feeling of culpability for another's misfortune, the emotional obsession with having done something wrong to another, is unproductive of a mature sense of responsibility for the fate of those who have been violated. Those who are rendered guilty by the act of witnessing violence against others are sometimes gripped by the feeling that they could easily disappear down a hole, chased by the anger, resentment or indignation of the violated. Even though their actions do not directly cause the suffering of the violated, the guilty feel the way they do because an inner voice tells them that they are indeed responsible. The guilty are haunted by the sound within themselves of the voice of judgement. They feel permanent unease at what they have done to others. That is why they themselves often fear retaliatory punishment or even inflict it upon themselves, for instance by means of permanent guilt.

In practice, among the witnesses of incivility and uncivil war, the emotions of guilt and shame are very often mixed together, but that does not void the distinction between them. Shame understandably arises in audiences when witnessing scenes of violence, but not simply because it is an emotion often connected with the process of seeing and being seen. Unlike the experience of guilt, in which the ego is neurotically haunted

---

[89] I am relying here on the suggestive formulations of Herbert Morris, 'Guilt and Shame', in *On Guilt and Innocence*, Berkeley, Calif. and Los Angeles 1976, pp. 59–63; Gabriele Taylor, *Pride, Shame and Guilt*, Oxford 1985; and Bernard Williams, *Shame and Necessity*, Berkeley, Calif., Los Angeles and London 1993, especially chapter 4.

and paralysed by the cries and blood of the violated, shame is initially the emotion of self-protection, in which the whole being of the shamed person seems diminished, but not obliterated. In their experience of shame, audiences are struck by their feeling of exposure to the violated, who themselves seem less angry and resentful (as in guilt) than contemptuous, derisive or dismissive of those who witness their plight. It is as if those who cry out or bleed are looking back at the audience and can see right through them, even though they are seated in safety, far away in the comfort of their living rooms and theatres; they feel exposed to the wrong people at the wrong time. Those who feel shame consequently are gripped by the desire to hide their faces, even the desire to switch off their television sets, or (like the first American cinema audiences to witness footage of concentration camp victims and survivors[90]) to disappear from the room. They feel shame not so much because of what they purportedly have done (as in guilt) but because they are gripped by the intuition that the violence they witness falls contemptibly short of the 'civilized' standards they expect of themselves and others in the world around them. Unlike the guilty, who wallow in the mire of their own guilt, weighed down by their urge to talk, to be listened to and to confess, those who are ashamed often will to recover or to improve themselves, and even to bond or interact with the violated. The experience of guilt always has a cut-and-dried threshold: an individual or group has either done wrong or not. Shame is by contrast a standard admitting of

---

90 Robert Abzug, *Inside the Vicious Heart: America and the Liberation of the Nazi Concentration Camps*, New York 1985, p. 170.

degrees of realization: the ashamed feel that they have failed to live up fully to a standard towards which they nevertheless still strive. The ashamed accordingly seek to decipher what has happened – sometimes for the purpose of rebuilding both themselves and the world in which they and their offspring have to live their future lives.

It is of interest that one of the first great twentieth-century novels about power and violence, Kafka's *The Trial*, ends with the theme of shame and not guilt. It might have been expected that the death scene, in which two officials stab Joseph K. twice through the heart in a deserted moonlit quarry, constitutes the pardon, the end of the interminable ordeal for the victim. Kafka refuses that ending by specifying that the shame of it all survives. 'Like a dog!' the victim splutters, vomiting his last words, as if he meant the shame of his murder to outlive him and to haunt posterity for ever. The whole scene is bleak, but here in literary form, surely, is a clue to one of the vital emotional responses required of thinking, judging, acting citizens everywhere to the plagues and images of violence that have blighted our century and marked it as the most unstable, dangerous and degrading phase of recorded human history. Genocidal wars, firebombed cities, nuclear explosions, concentration camps, orgies of private blood-letting: Should we too not feel ashamed of what we have done to each other during this long century of violence?

Further Reading

Although contemporary political theory has little to say about the subject, the twentieth-century history of philosophical and political reflections on violence is a rich collage of conflicting and converging insights. A number of these remain vital in any assessment of the contours of this sad century of violence. For their helpful suggestions about how to interpret this material, astute criticisms of earlier drafts of this essay and energetic help in its preparation, I should like to thank the following friends, family and colleagues: Rebecca Allison, Patrick Burke, Barry Buzan, Gabriela Cerruti, Jeremy Colwill, Juan Corradi, Jane Hindle, Livio Hughes, Malcolm Imrie, Tomaž Mastnak, Anna Matveeva, Paul Mier, Chantal Mouffe, Kathy O'Neil, Vukašin Pavlović, Isobel Rorison, Chris Sparks, Derek Summerfield and Azzam Tamimi. Readers who remain unsatisfied with the material cited in this essay and who are interested in deepening their understanding of the subject may wish to consult the following additional literature on violence written at different moments during this century by specialists in various academic disciplines.

Alfred Adler, 'La Guerre et l'état primitif', in Miguel Abensour, ed., *L'Esprit des lois sauvages: Pierre Clastres ou une nouvelle anthropologie politique*, Paris 1987.

J.K. Anderson, *Military Practice and Theory in the Age of Xenophon*, Berkeley, Calif. 1970.

R. K. Betts, 'Nuclear Weapons and Conventional War', *Journal of Strategic Studies* 11 (March 1988), pp. 79–95.

H. Bonet, *The Tree of Battles*, Liverpool 1949.

Ian Buruma, *The Wages of Guilt. Memories of War in Germany and Japan*, London 1995.

Barry Buzan, *People, States and Fear. An Agenda for International Security Studies in the Post-Cold War Era*, 2nd edn, New York, London, Toronto, Sydney, Tokyo and Singapore 1991.

R. Caillois, 'Le Vertige de la guerre', in *Quatre essais de sociologie contemporaine*, Paris 1951.

Peter Calvocoressi and Guy Wint, *Total War*, London 1972.

Carlo M. Cipolla, *Guns and Sails in the Early Phase of European Expansion 1500–1700*, London 1965.

C. von Clausewitz, *On War*, M. Howard and P. Paret, eds, Princeton, N.J. 1976.

Jeremy Colwill, 'From Nuremberg to Bosnia and Beyond: War Crimes Trials in the Modern Era', *Social Justice*, volume 22, number 3 (1995).

John Crichton, ed., *Psychiatric Patient Violence. Risk and Response*, London 1995.

C. Duby, *The Chivalrous Society*, Berkeley, Calif. 1977.

Norbert Elias, *The Loneliness of the Dying*, Oxford and Cambridge, Mass. 1985.

Norbert Elias and Eric Dunning, *Quest for Excitement. Sport and Leisure in the Civilizing Process*, Oxford and Cambridge, Mass. 1993.

Jean Bethke Elshtain, *Women and War*, Chicago and London 1995.

Samuel E. Finer, 'State and Nation-Building in Europe: the Role of the Military', in Charles Tilly, ed., *The*

Formation of National States in Western Europe, Princeton, N.J. 1975.

Michel Foucault, *Discipline and Punish. The Birth of the Prison*, London 1977.

Richard J. Gelles, 'Physical Violence, Child Abuse, and Child Violence: A Continuum of Violence, or Distinct Behaviours?', *Human Nature*, volume 2, number 1 (1991), pp. 59–72.

René Girard, *Violence and the Sacred*, Baltimore, Md 1977.

René Girard, 'Generative Violence and the Extinction of Social Order', *Salmagundi*, 63–4 (Spring–Summer 1984), pp. 204–37.

Stephen P. Halbrook, *That Every Man Be Armed: The Evolution of a Constitutional Right*, Albuquerque, N.M. 1984.

J. Hale, 'War and Public Opinion in Renaissance Italy', in E.R. Jacob, ed., *Italian Renaissance Studies*, New York 1960.

Pierre Hassner, 'Beyond the Three Traditions: The Philosophy of War and Peace in Historical Perspective', *International Affairs* 70, number 4 (1994), pp. 737–56.

Johan Huizinga, 'The Political and Military Significance of Chivalric Ideas in the Late Middle Ages', in *Men and Ideas. History, the Middle Ages, the Renaissance. Essays by Johan Huizinga*, New York 1959.

Lynne Jones, *The Process of Engagement in Non-Violent Collective Action,* unpublished Ph.D dissertation, University of Bath 1995.

Ernst Jünger, *In Stahlgewittern*, Berlin 1931.

Mary Kaldor, *The Baroque Arsenal*, New York 1982.

John Keane, 'Despotism and Democracy. The Origins and Development of the Distinction Between Civil

Society and the State, 1750–1850', in John Keane, ed., *Civil Society and the State. New European Perspectives*, London and New York 1988.

M. Keen, *Chivalry*, New Haven 1984.

Herbert C. Kelman, 'Violence without Moral Restraint: Reflections on the Dehumanization of Victims and Victimizers', *Journal of Social Issues*, volume 29, number 4 (1973), pp. 25–61.

Walter Kendrick, *The Thrill of Fear: 250 Years of Scary Entertainment*, New York 1991.

Carl Leiden and Karl M. Schmitt, *The Politics of Violence: Revolution in the Modern World*, Englewood Cliffs, N.J. 1968.

René Lemarchand, *Burundi. Ethnocide as Discourse and Practice*, Cambridge 1994.

Jeremy McBride, 'Protection of Human Rights and Fundamental Freedoms in the Economies in Transition: The Role of the Council of Europe', unpublished paper, Moscow 1995.

Jock McCulloch, *Black Soul, White Artifact. Fanon's Clinical Psychology and Social Theory*, Cambridge and New York 1983.

Joyce Lee Malcolm, *To Keep and Bear Arms: The Origins of an Anglo-American Right*, Cambridge, Mass. 1994.

Michael Mallett, *Mercenaries and their Masters: Warfare in Renaissance Italy*, London 1974.

Edward D. Mansfield and Jack Snyder, 'Democratization and War', *Foreign Affairs*, volume 74, number 3 (May/June 1995), pp. 79–97.

Gary T. Marx, *Undercover: Police Surveillance in America*, New York 1988.

Gary T. Marx, *Civil Disorder and the Agents of Social Control*, Irvington 1993.

Tomaž Mastnak, *Christendom, Europe, and the Muslims*,

unpublished manuscript, Ljubljana 1995.

Paul Mier, John Keane and Alberto Melucci, 'New Perspectives on Social Movements: An Interview', in John Keane and Paul Mier, eds, *Nomads of the Present*, London and Philadelphia 1989.

Larry Minear and Thomas G. Weiss, *Mercy Under Fire. War and the Global Humanitarian Community*, Boulder, Colo., San Francisco and Oxford 1995.

Jean-Luc Nancy, 'Violence et violence', *lignes*, number 25 (May 1995), pp. 293–8.

Peter Paret, *Understanding War. Essays on Clausewitz and the History of Military Power*, Princeton, N.J. 1992.

C. Phillipson, *The International Law and Custom of Ancient Greece and Rome*, London 1911.

Daniel Pick, *War Machine. The Rationalisation of Slaughter in the Modern Age*, New Haven and London 1993.

R.A. Preston, S.F. Wise, and H.O. Werner, *Men in Arms: A History of Warfare and its Interrelationships with Western Society*, London 1956.

Clayton A. Robarchek, 'Primitive Warfare and the Ratomorphic Image of Mankind', *American Anthropologist* 91 (1989), pp. 903–20.

Lois G. Schwoerer, *'No Standing Armies!' The Antiarmy Ideology in Seventeenth Century England*, Baltimore, Md 1974.

Patricia Searles and Ronald J. Berger, eds, *Rape and Society. Readings on the Problem of Sexual Assault*, Boulder, Colo., San Francisco and Oxford 1995.

Edmond Silberner, *La Guerre dans la pensée économique du XVI au XVIII siècle*, Paris 1939.

Arnold J. Toynbee, *War and Civilization*, London, New York and Toronto 1951.

J.P. Vernant, ed., *Problèmes de la guerre en Grèce ancienne*, Paris 1968.

Kenneth N. Waltz, *Man, the State and War: A Theoretical Analysis*, New York 1959.

Michael Walzer, *Just and Unjust Wars: A Moral Argument with Historical Illustrations*, New York 1977.

Glenn D. Wolfner and Richard J. Gelles, 'A Profile of Violence Towards Children: A National Study', *Child Abuse & Neglect*, volume 17 (1993), pp. 197–212.

Sheldon Wolin, 'Violence and the Western Political Tradition', *American Journal of Orthopsychiatry*, volume 33 (1963), pp. 15–28.

Index

Entries in **bold** indicate individual sections in this volume; 'n' indicates a footnote reference.

Index